To Wayne—

for me.
Best wishes,
Mike
(a.k.a. Michael S. Pritchard)

Golf Lessons

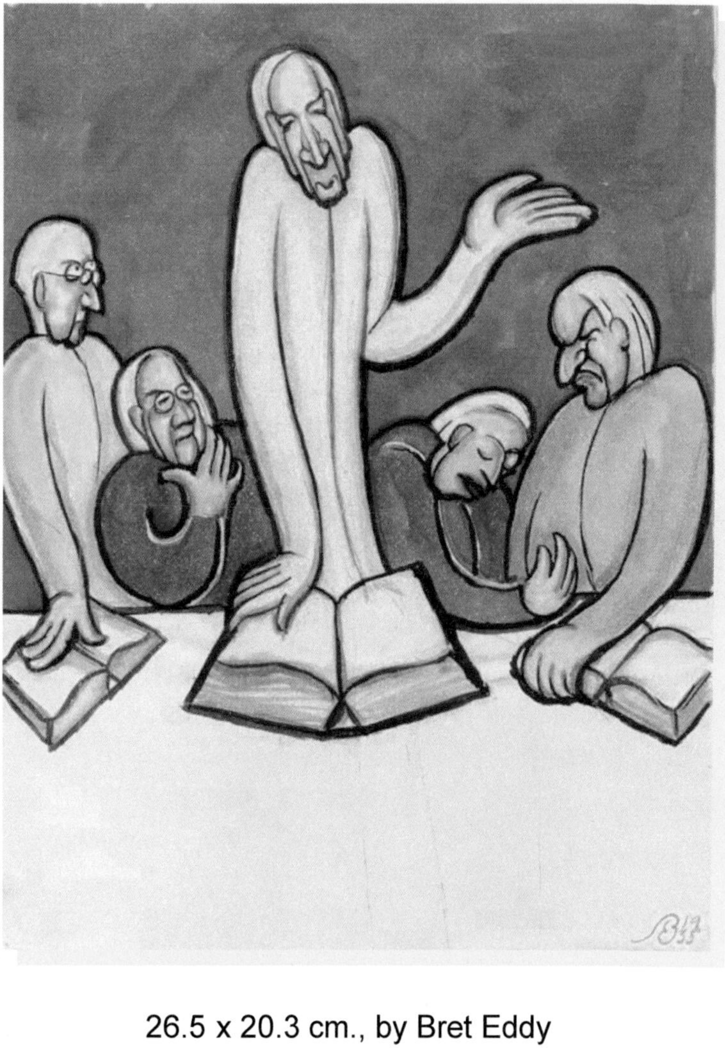

26.5 x 20.3 cm., by Bret Eddy

Golf Lessons

Links to Life

by

Michael S. Pritchard

Buttonwood Press 2004

Buttonwood Press, L.L.C.
P.O. Box 716
Hazlett, MI 48840

Pritchard, Michael S. (1941-)
Golf lessons: links to life. / Haslett, MI: / Buttonwood Press, / 2004.
xiv, 294 p.
1. Pritchard, Michael S.—Biography 2. Philosophy teachers—United States—Michigan 3. Golf—Biography 4. Kalamazoo County (Mich.)—Biography I. Title
B945 .P75 191 .P75

ISBN: 0-9742920-1-X
Printed by Fidlar Doubleday, Inc.
Kalamazoo, Michigan

DEDICATION

Golf Lessons is dedicated to my brother, Peter Eddy Pritchard. Peter looms large in many of these little stories. As his younger brother, I often felt as if I were living in his shadow. This is something I sought to overcome, not by diminishing Peter's shadow, but by standing alongside it.

Sure, when I was four years old, he told me that ghosts reside in the bodies of our neighbor's cows—and that they might leave those bodies and come after me if I lingered on the way home from school. But this was his way of protecting me. As a fourth grader, Peter had to stay in school all day. As a kindergartner, I had to leave for home at noon. It was a one-mile walk back to our grandparents' little farm. They worried that I might get hurt playing in the gravel pit along the way, and Peter was instructed to encourage me to go straight home. So, he fed my imagination with his own.

Sure, he used to tell me, "It's Cheeri Oats, stupid, not Cheery Os," when as a little tyke I'd say I wanted Cheery Os for breakfast. Then, to his chagrin, he discovered that General Mills had actually changed the name of our favorite cereal to Cheerios. Apparently I was too young to remember this, but he finally told me about it when I was 61.

Sure, he got angry with me when I threw the baseball beyond his reach, and he'd tell me I'd never be a real ball player. But he was probably only dishing out to me what our father, a superb athlete with demandingly high standards, had dished out to him.

Sure, he was a high school "big shot," while I was a junior high "pip–squeak". But as I moved through high school, he introduced me to his college friends as his younger brother who was on his high school basketball team. He added that he hadn't made his high school team. But he didn't tell them that I sat on the bench of a team that lost nearly all its games, and that he very nearly made his high school team, one of the best in the state.

Sure, I never got to go to BobLo Island, and he never let me wear his BobLo sailor hat. But he did give me his set of Gorman irons when he went off to college. And he helped buy me a new set of Gormans during my college years when the old Gormans gave out.

I may have been his little brother, but at age sixteen I was Peter's best man when he and Penny married at age twenty-one. A year later they named their first son Michael. And Peter bought me a wedding suit when, at twenty-one, I married Millie.

A pretty good shadow to try to stand alongside, I'd say.

TABLE OF CONTENTS

Getting Started

Golf Lessons

There is more to life than golf. Even the most fanatical golfer must accept this. Many of my best friends have never even swung a golf club. They may not know what they are missing, but they don't care. Who am I to say that their lives are less satisfying than Arnold Palmer's? Besides, even fanatics have to eat, sleep, and watch television. In my own case, I know I had a reasonably good life before I made my fateful decision to take up golf at age thirteen.

However, I don't want to talk about such truisms. There is also more to golf than golf. That's what I want to talk about.

I don't recommend that anyone take up the game of golf—at least, I don't do this anymore. How, then, can I approve of *my* playing golf? I'm not necessarily *opposed* to others taking up the game. I think I can pass Immanuel Kant's great moral test, his famous Categorical Imperative: I play golf. Can I will it to be a Universal Law that everyone play golf? Yes, I can. But my Universal Law is permissive, not mandatory. It's not that I think everyone *ought* to take up the game. I'm not sure even *I* ought to have taken it up. Things might have turned out much better for me if I hadn't. But I doubt it.

No, my Universal Law goes like this: As far as I'm concerned, anyone who really *wants* to take up the game may do so. Of course, I could change my mind. If too many want to play, I'll support restrictions. Seniority will then be my rule. My first round of golf was in June 1954. So, if the courses I want to play get too crowded, I'll will it to be a Universal Law that anyone who took up the game in June 1954 or earlier may play on those courses if they want to. Everyone else can stand in line or go away.

Golf is often thought of as a game for elites. It is. But it isn't just for elites. Or at least it wasn't from 1954 to 1963. Of the hundreds of rounds of golf I played during those years, I probably paid for no more than a dozen. That's fortunate, since I'm not sure how I was able to find the money even for those. Besides, by 1963 Arnold Palmer had made the game popular, and elites and non-elites alike flocked to the golf courses—albeit, sorting themselves into those who could afford the posh private clubs and those, like me, who settled for the hard-panned public links.

My free golf came from many sources: my parents, caddying, playing on my high school and college golf teams, working summers as a groundskeeper on a golf course, bartending, and even one spring of coaching a golf team. The stories that follow are as much about what I've learned from my family, my teachers, caddying, groundskeeping, bartending, and coaching as from hitting golf balls. That's part of what I mean by saying that not all of golf is about golf.

But I've learned about a lot more than hitting golf balls by hitting golf balls. That's also part of what I mean. No doubt there are others parts of what I mean, too—parts I don't fully understand (and never will). But it's time to begin—at the beginning.

In the Beginning

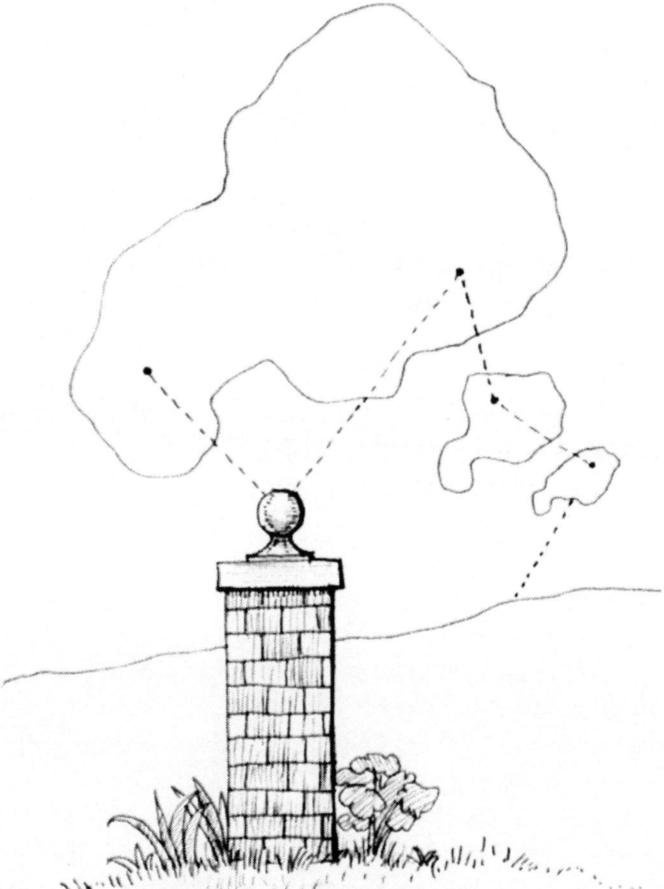

In the Beginning

From the very first I knew golf was. . .well, *boring*. We moved from my grandparents' small farm to Saginaw, Michigan, when I was five. To reassure me that even city life can embrace open fields, my parents used take me to Rolling Green Golf Course. I never understood why it was called *rolling* green. It was flat as a pancake.

However, my greatest disappointment at Rolling Green was trying to hit practice balls with my first set of golf clubs. Of course, cotton practice balls don't go far even when hit with a regular golf club. But my 20-inch clubs were hopeless. Even real golf balls wouldn't go more than a few inches.

Still, I loved that first set of clubs—at least when swinging them in our hotel room. I fell in love with them the first time I saw them in the five-and-dime store across the street from the Bancroft Hotel, our residence during the summer of my fifth year. What really impressed me was that they looked *real*. The irons had black leather-like grips, wooden shafts, and nickel-plated heads—with real grooves! Nothing like the plastic imitations I presented to our children some 25 years later. The practice balls left something to be desired, fuzzy cotton balls that flattened out when you squeezed them. And they weren't nearly as tasty as real golf balls.

But the clubs—they looked *authentic*, as authentic as my favorite toy pistols. I always preferred realistic looking toys, just like I preferred Randolph Scott and Alan Ladd to Roy Rogers and Gene Autry. Give me a cowboy who knows how to lose a fight once in a while.

I never wanted a real six-shooter, even though I had no tolerance for the really fakey looking toy guns. (For a while I did want a Red Ryder BB rifle, but probably only because it *looked* more like a real rifle than my imitations.) After a summer at Rolling Green, I was sure I'd never want a set of real golf clubs either. Playing at playing golf would be quite enough. Like playing with toy guns, I would outgrow my toy clubs. I would be free from both the toys and the real things. But by the time I was thirteen, I learned I was only half right.

Farm Lessons

L.H. Eddy was my grandfather and my first idol. He always seemed to have something to say about everything. He lectured my parents and older brother about what's worthwhile, how to make a good living, and cow-pasture pool.

I could tell that my parents and brother didn't like what he told them. They made that clear on the way back home from our visits to my grandparents' farm. The fact that they didn't tell *him* that they didn't appreciate his lectures impressed me. They certainly told *me* when they'd heard enough from me.

Only Ethel "Dolly" Eddy, his wife of 60 plus years, had the nerve to tell L.H. Eddy we'd *all* heard quite enough. But that was years later. By then he was into his nineties. It seemed so easy, "Oh shut up, Lawrence. No one wants to hear what you have to say." To everyone's surprise, he did shut up. For the last few years of his life he contented himself by looking out the window at birds.

It would have taken a lot more than that to get

L.H. Eddy to shut up when he was in his sixties. That's when he was determined to set everyone straight—and wasn't about to take any nos, buts, or maybes. That's also when I sat at his feet, thoroughly enjoying his telling my parents and brother a thing or two!

So, when he tried to set everyone straight about cow-pasture pool, I listened. "Cow-pasture pool, that's all it is," he said. Thrusting his hands toward the field across the road, he'd laugh loudly and complete his little lecture, "Silly game—hitting a little ball with a stick out there where the cows belong."

Nevertheless, we always seemed to have a set of golf clubs in the trunk of the car when visiting our grandparents' little farm. Maybe my parents and brother didn't like what L.H. Eddy had to say about cow-pasture pool. But, why would they bring their clubs along if they didn't think they'd learn something from him about golf?

So, they asked for it—and he didn't disappoint them. They were good golfers. My father frequently shot below par. Yet, there was L.H. Eddy telling him how to improve his swing. He'd never hit a golf ball in his life. But it didn't matter. How tough could it be to hit a little white ball in a cow pasture?

"If you want a challenge," he'd say, "try my bow and arrow." He'd hang a target over a pile of hay, get out his homemade bow, and watch me struggle to get the arrow to drop just past my feet. Then L.H. Eddy would shoot a few bull's-eyes and walk away chortling. If he was so much on target with a bow and arrow, I wondered, how could he be wrong about golf? My brother clinched it.

One day at the farm he let me swing his 5-iron. As a right-hander, I first took a few swipes from the right side. Then I turned the club around and took a few more from the left side.

"Hey everybody, come here," Peter called out. "Look at Mike. His left-handed swing is better than his right-handed one!" I took that as a deep compliment. Here I was, nine years old, a true novice, and I had mastered switch-swinging without even hitting a ball. "Grandpa's right," I thought, "this game is *too* easy." Why bother with such a simple sport when there are so many others to humiliate me?

So, I stayed away from golf and concentrated on baseball, basketball, and football until I was thirteen. Only much later did I figure out that I had misunderstood Peter's "compliment." Maybe my left-handed swing was better. But either way, he must have thought, it's just a matter of degree—of hopelessness.

Ignoring my grandfather's dismissal of golf, I took up the game at age thirteen. Just possibly he was right all along. When he followed Dolly Eddy's advice and receded into silence, everyone feared the worst—senility had set in. But his exile may have been self-imposed. Conversation at Easter dinner in 1974 turned to Republican President Richard Nixon and the Watergate fiasco. After much discussion, a voice not heard for nearly two years joined in: "Nixon's an ass, always was, and always will be," said 95-year old L.H. Eddy, a lifelong Republican who couldn't resist having the last word.

Now Coach?

Neck Springs

Although my parents and older brother were avid golfers, there was little they could do to persuade me that golf was anything other than boring. Baseball was for me. A nifty uniform, never mind its woolen itchiness. A nifty baseball cap, never mind the sweat dripping on my glasses. A nifty glove, with its well-grooved pocket and tasty buckskin laces.

Let them play their boring game, I thought. How could hitting a stationary ball be challenging? Hitting a moving baseball—now there was a challenge! Each season my coaches had high expectations for me, only to be mystified by my ineptness at bat. I was told I had a smooth, fluid swing. I could hit the ball as far as anyone on the team, as long as I tossed it up in the air for myself. Anything thrown by someone else was another matter.

Fastballs terrorized me, but it was the curve ball that really did me in. How embarrassing to jump back from a ball coming right at me, only to watch it swoop in for a strike—or to relax the bat on my shoulder while watching a ball a mile outside work its way back over the plate. The key to my utter failure was this: I simply couldn't see the ball well enough to hit it. I had *too many* eyes, the shared misfortune of many stuck with the epithet, "Four Eyes".

Perhaps I could have fared better as a pitcher. I had a hard, if errant, fastball. In the only inning I ever pitched, I struck out the other team's best hitter, no doubt because he sensed that the two fastballs I threw in the direction of his head were quite unintentional. I retired the side without a hit. Unfortunately, three walks and a ground ball between the shortstop's legs brought in two runs.

I realized that matters would only become worse. Soon I would have to move up a level to the 13–14 year-old league. It was not something to which I could look forward. Clearly I needed an excuse to get out of baseball.

It was provided by, of all people, Irving Oswalt Menzel, head coach of Traverse City Central High School's football team. If there was any sport I played worse than baseball, it was football. Eighth grade football taught me true cowardice. I made the mistake of tackling the star runner's knee with my head. I suddenly understood the meaning of the expression, “seeing stars”. From then on I found that the rest of my body followed my head as I tried to avoid banging it against on-rushing knees.

Coach Thompson tried gently to convince me that football wasn't for everybody. Of course, he didn't have an older brother on the high school team. I wasn't about to quit and have Peter call me a chicken-livered coward, even if I was one.

"Coach Menzel really likes to scare kids in gym class," said my brother when he found out who my eighth grade gym teacher was. "He squeezes everybody into the balcony on the first day. Then he yells so loud his voice bounces off the ceiling and all the walls at once."

Noticing that I'd begun to tremble slightly, he offered some reassuring words, "Don't worry—he doesn't mean it when he screams that you're the lowest form of life on earth and that you'll be in his class *forever* if you can't pass all the physical requirements."

"He doesn't?" I asked incredulously. I had already seen Coach Irving Oswalt Menzel in action. My brother was a senior on the toughest, meanest high school football team in northern Michigan. And Coach Menzel was the toughest, meanest coach I'd ever seen.

"Well, you do have to pass the requirements. But there are only two tough ones—neck springs and rope climbing. And you only have to do one of those." As Peter spoke I looked down at my spindly arms and legs, quickly surmising that rope climbing was out of the question.

"*Neck springs*! What are they?" I asked in desperation.

"Tough stuff. You lie on a mat and roll back on your neck with your legs pulled up to your chest. With your hands behind your head, you spring forward, arch your back, and land on your feet. Hardly anybody can do it. You'd better go for the rope climb. You just have to pull yourself up about 20 feet. The only trick is that you can't use your legs."

"I can't do *that*. Look at me—5' 2", 108 pounds, glasses. Besides, it's not fair, I'm only twelve. I started school a year early. Can't I get out of it?"

"Sure, stupid. Go back to the seventh grade!"

I wasn't about to go back to Mr. H.O. Yank's seventh grade. He'd already caused me enough trouble. When he told the class about South American cock fights, those of us who couldn't suppress a few snickers were called into his office. Now wearing his principal's hat, he demanded: "Well, young men, just *what* was so amusing?" All we offered were our silent, beet-red faces.

Mr. H.O. Yank never laughed, not even when Lance Neuman reported to the class that his mother and sister had bought lots of interesting things at the "local brassiere". No sense of humor, that man.

Obviously he had something against boys. He made us go out in the playground so the girls could watch a movie by themselves. We were warned that anyone caught trying to look through the window would be *very* sorry.

"No way," I told Peter. "I'm staying in the eighth grade!"

"Stay in the eighth grade then, but not *too* long. I'd better not hear any stories about my little brother flunking Coach's gym class. If you think Menzel's tough, try me!"

"Cut it out, Peter. If you even come *close* to me, I'll tell Mom and Dad."

"Right, Mr. Tattletale. When are you going to learn to stand up for yourself? Grow up. Look at me. I'm the skinniest lineman on the football team. I don't take crap from anybody. That's why I'm on the first team. Coach Menzel likes guys with guts. If a skinny guy like me can do it, so can you."

Somehow Peter's urgings didn't offer me much encouragement. I stared at his bulging biceps and his taut, 5' 10", 160-pound frame. Looking around to make sure help was within earshot, I replied, "You think you're so big and tough. I can hardly wait to grow up. As soon as I'm big enough, I'll knock your block off."

Such bravado! If I was certain of *anything* at age twelve, it was that I would never be big enough to knock off my brother's block.

I made sure my friends were properly informed of Menzel the Menace before the first day of our lives as eighth graders. After all, we were going to be in junior high now. I thought it only fair that they share my terror.

Absolute fear of failure and certainty that I could never rope climb must have given me an extra shot of adrenaline. I mastered the neck spring almost immediately. As I watched my classmates repeatedly land on their bottoms, I marveled at my good fortune. How had I found it so easy? I had no idea, but I wasn't going to press my luck by trying the rope climb.

Actually, I hoped that somehow I would survive gym class without Coach Menzel even noticing me. His student assistant could mark down that I passed the neck-spring test. I would then make myself as inconspicuous as possible. No such luck. The assistant made a point of bringing the coach over to watch me neck spring. To my great surprise and embarrassment, Coach Menzel asked me to demonstrate my technique to the rest of the class!

I've never really understood why I was able to do a neck spring or why so many of my classmates were not. But, then, I've never understood why I'm able to stiffen all my fingers and bend them only at the knuckles closest to my fingertips or why hardly anyone else I know can. I discovered I could perform this little trick when I was seven. One of my brother's friends tried to impress me by holding up his oddly bent forefinger and saying, "Here's something you can't do."

"You mean this?" I said, as I held up eight even more oddly bent fingers—much to the surprise of both of us.

In any case, I was grateful for my newly discovered ability. I was still a 5' 2", 108-pound weakling. I still knew I couldn't climb even one-third of the way up that 20-foot rope. But I knew I could do a neck spring. And I knew that Coach Irving Oswalt Menzel knew I could do a neck spring. I discovered that I felt a lot better about myself and a lot better about Coach Irving Oswalt Menzel.

So, naturally, I listened with great interest when Coach Menzel announced that the Traverse City Country Club needed caddies. Good caddies, he said, are attentive, courteous, dependable, and hard-working. Caddying, he added, is a good way to learn how to become a responsible worker and make some money.

A wise man, Coach Menzel. He knew just the right words to lure Bruce, George, Lance, and me to the golf course. I had my excuse to give up baseball. It was time to learn how to be a responsible worker and make a little money. It never dawned on me that I was taking a fateful step. Soon I would discover that, whatever else can be said against it, golf is not boring for those caught in its snare.

Caddyshack

To be a caddy, I'd have to give up my other job. Big decision time. Do I continue delivering the *Traverse City Record Eagle* or do I make big bucks at the Traverse City Country Club?

Would I miss getting ink all over my hands every day while folding and stuffing 118 papers into my filthy paperbag and delivering them to 118 different doorsteps? Would I miss having customers yell at me for throwing their papers into their bushes and water sprinklers instead of on their porches? Or for throwing papers against their doors instead of setting them gently on their doormats?

Which would I prefer? Knocking on 118 doors each month to beg my customers to pay me so that I wouldn't fall short on my bill for the third straight month? Or having cold cash plunked in my palm immediately after each caddying job without having to give up *any* of it to *anyone*?

Silly questions!

So Bruce, George, Lance, and I showed up at the caddyshack as soon as we were released from the 8th grade. Unfortunately, so did about 50 other kids—*big* kids. And about 20 golfers.

"Listen up, little birdies," said the caddymaster to the first-time caddies. "The early birdies get the worms. The worms are what's left after the experienced caddies have their jobs." Very educational, a practical introduction to seniority. We had a very long first day "on the job". It was an even longer second day for the four early birdies.

"Don't worry, little birdies," reassured the caddymaster. "Rome wasn't built in a day, not even two days. Everybody gets to caddy on Saturday. Just make sure you're here by 6:00 A.M. sharp!"

At least there was a lot of talk in the caddyshack. Loud talk. Loud, *dirty* talk. So loud and dirty that my father couldn't help but hear it when he walked by one day.

That evening my parents expressed their concerns. My father said that was the *worst* language he'd ever heard. My mother said she certainly hoped *I* wasn't one of the boys my father heard. I said that I *heard* some of that awful talk, but *I* certainly didn't talk that way. (Why is it that we remember our lies so much longer than anything else we say?)

Then my father planted the seeds for my escape from the job that Coach Menzel told us would reward attentive, courteous, dependable, hard-working young men by helping them become responsible workers and by putting some money in their pockets. "Maybe," he said, "you shouldn't be a caddy. I don't think it's a good idea for you to hang around a bunch of foul-mouthed kids."

"It's not so bad, Dad," I replied. "You just hear the loud ones. Everybody isn't like *that*." Right, I added to myself, some of us aren't *loud* dirty talkers—just *dirty* talkers. But I knew that if I ever got my fill of dirty talk, I had a ready-made excuse for quitting.

I soon seized the opportunity. Caddying turned out to be as boring as it was infrequent. Beginning caddies always seemed to get stuck with beginning golfers. Within a week Lance and I were the only ones left in our quartet. All of us suspected we could play better than the people whose bags we lugged around the course. Having lost all respect for the game, Bruce told us he was taking up tennis. George simply didn't show up at the caddyshack anymore.

Meanwhile, Lance and I became more and more convinced that we could play better than anyone we caddied for, even though neither of us had ever hit a golf ball. Then it happened. There was George, *playing* golf with his next door neighbor, Bucky.

"What are you guys doing?" shouted Lance.

"What's it look like, stupid?" replied George.

"It's hard to tell," I laughed.

"I told you I could play better than those old duffers," George snarled. "Watch this." We watched George take a mighty swoop at the ball which dribbled a full 75 yards down the fairway. "Top that!" he gloated.

"We would," said Lance, "but we're *caddies*. So are you, George. You're not supposed to be playing. Wait 'til they catch you!"

"Don't you guys know anything? Haven't you ever heard of *family* memberships? Kids can play everyday after 3:00 P.M. I've been playing with Bucky for the last week, and look how I'm hitting already."

"You call 75 yards *hitting* it?"

"You betcha. I can hit it 110 when I really *want* to. But Bucky hits it 125 every time. 'Course he's in his second year. Show 'em, Bucky."

Bucky smoothly cut across the ball, sending a low line drive slicing 125 yards into the right rough. "You guys couldn't do that in a *100* years," snorted George. That hurt. Bucky was just going *into* the eighth grade. I ignored the fact that Bucky and I were actually the same age. Had he ever been knocked silly by a star halfback's right knee? And he probably hadn't even heard of Coach Irving Menzel yet. Lance and I, on the other hand, were *survivors*.

Lance and I looked at each other. Why hadn't we thought of it before? Family memberships. Both of our families belonged to the Traverse City Country Club.

Suddenly we realized we were going to hit golf balls 126 yards—even if it took us all summer!

We answered George's challenge with the cleverest caddyshack obscenities we could muster up, calling for a duel at the earliest opportunity.

My parents were relieved to learn that evening that I would no longer be frequenting the foul-mouthed caddyshack. But they were stunned to hear me ask if I could borrow somebody's clubs for a big match tomorrow. How is it, they wondered, that after all those years of turning up my nose at golf, suddenly I wanted to get my hands on some golf clubs?

"I don't know. I just *have* to play golf."

First Clubs

To play golf, I needed some clubs. My father had a few he no longer used. There was a 7-iron with a warped, wooden shaft, an 8-iron with a bamboo shaft that was just beginning to splinter, a 3-wood whose head was coming loose, a driver that even my father found difficult to control, a couple of other mismatched irons, a blade putter, and a blond 4-wood that worked so well that I hated to part with it when I purchased my four persimmon woods a few years later.

Fortunately, it wasn't long before I inherited a newer set of clubs.

Although my father was playing very little golf at the time, he decided to enter the Traverse City Club Championship in the summer of 1954. He hadn't played much that summer because of painful bouts of bursitis in his back, so his game wasn't sharp enough to qualify for the Championship Flight. Instead, he was placed in the First Flight. He asked me to caddy for him, my first and only opportunity to watch him play competitive golf. At the end of the day he walked out of the clubhouse carrying a set of new Chick Harbert clubs, his prize for taking first place in his flight.

As I recall, his score was somewhere in the mid-70s, just a few over par. Still, he was upset with a chip that fell short of the green on the second hole, a skied drive on the tenth, and a couple of other shots that didn't meet his high standards.

Back still bothering him, my father gave his new clubs to my brother Peter, who took them with him to the University of Michigan that fall. In turn, Peter gave me the irons he used as No. 1 man on Traverse City High School's golf team.

I now had six fully-matched Gorman irons and a Tommy Armour 6-iron bearing the signature of the author of my first guide to golf, *How to Play Your Best Golf All the Time*. Peter acquired these clubs when we lived in Saginaw, purchasing them with his earnings from delivering *The Saginaw News*. He also spent $12 for six golf lessons from Frank Pegler, the pro at Rolling Green Golf Course.

Bucky, George, Lance, and I played golf together as much as we could, but I thought I might pick up a tip or two from my brother and mother, too. So I asked if I could join them for a round. I ogled at Peter's powerful shots. However, I was not nearly discerning enough. Any line drive was a marvel to me. Peter hit a clothesline 3-wood down the left side, far left of his intended target. I made the mistake of telling him how impressed I was with this, and I was stunned to see him boiling in anger and to find myself on the receiving end of much of it.

"You don't know anything about this game. Don't *ever* try to tell me that a shot like that's any good!" On the next hole my mother shanked a shot into my shin. I quickly concluded that it would be wiser to stick with my buddies.

Creative Computing

I began playing serious golf in the summer of 1954 at the Traverse City Country Club. I don't remember any particular shots I made that summer of my thirteenth year. However, I do remember my lowest score for nine holes, 59. I don't really know how I managed to get such a low score. All my others were 70 or worse (*much* worse). Perhaps it was one of my rounds with Bucky. Maybe it went something like this:

Bucky: [After hitting a bad drive and teeing up another ball,] Mulligan!

Mike: Mulligan? What's that?

Bucky: It means I get to hit a second ball. The first one doesn't count.

Mike: You hit it, didn't you? Why doesn't it count?

Bucky: Because it's a Mulligan. Everyone's entitled to a Mulligan.

Mike: [After hitting a terrible second shot and dropping another ball to hit,] Mulligan!

Bucky: You can't have a Mulligan. You get Mulligan's only on your first shot.

Mike: That's not fair. I didn't know that. Besides you already had one, so now I get one.

Bucky: Fairness doesn't matter. Rules do.

Mike: Hey, it's just a game. We can make up our own rules, *fair* ones.

Bucky: A rule's a rule.

Mike: Rule, schmule. We're just learning. We need *practice*. Let's play two balls and keep track of how we do with each!

Bucky: Well, okay, but just today. I guess we do need practice.

Mike: [After hitting a lousy shot with his second ball,] I think I'll hit a second ball for my second ball.

Bucky: [After topping the second ball for his second ball,] I'm going to hit a second ball for my second ball for my second ball.

Mike: [After topping the second ball for his second ball for his second ball,] I'm going to hit a second ball for my second ball for my second ball for my second ball.

Bucky: I'm out of balls. Can you lend me one so I can hit a second ball for my fourth second ball?

Mike: [Much later, after hitting at least a half-dozen second balls,] This last one's a gimme. So, I'll just pick it up.

Bucky: Whadja get?

Mike: Six.

Bucky: No way! Did you count your gimme?

Mike: Count my gimme? Why should do that? I didn't have to hit it; it was a *gimme*.

Bucky: You have to count your gimmies, just like your whiffs. It doesn't matter if you don't hit the ball.

Mike: That doesn't seem fair. Why count what you don't hit?

Bucky: I told you, what's fair doesn't matter. It's the *rules*. Besides, I *know* you got more than 6. You hit a ton of shots.

Mike: But most of them were *seconds*. Do you mean I have to count all the seconds, too? That's a crazy rule.

Bucky: No, you count your *first* ball. How many times did you hit your first ball? I'll bet it was at least
ten times.

Mike: Get serious. I couldn't keep track of all those balls. They were all first balls for me. That's how you're supposed to practice. Be serious about every shot, my brother says. Treat 'em all like they count, but you just said I don't have to count all of them. So, what do I do now?

Bucky: How should I know? *You* made up the rule.

Mike: Right! It's *best* ball. Whenever I hit two balls from the same spot I take the best one for my score. The other one doesn't count. Like I said, I got 6—plus the gimme, I guess. This is great. Let's play best of three balls on the next hole.

Bucky: Not if we're going to finish number seven before the sun goes down!

This is what I call *creative computing*—another of the many lessons I've learned from golf. Golf can do wonders for your math, if only you're willing to take a shot in the dark.

Maybe I Can't Boogie, But I Sure Can Bogie

I danced before I golfed. Eighth graders were allowed to attend dances at Traverse City High School, so I stepped on the dance floor at age twelve, several months before joining Lance, George and Bucky on the golf course. I still golf, but I almost never dance. Worse, for years I've proclaimed to others that I *cannot* dance, even though when I watch others I know I *could*, if I really tried.

Trying's the rub—getting up in front of others and pretending I know what I'm doing when I really don't. Surely others will see how inept I am. If I'm going to dance, I have to get it *right*.

Oddly, this hasn't stopped me from golfing. I've never had a golf lesson. I don't videotape my swing. I just play and hope that no one detects a fatal flaw. I work hard at trying to minimize dubs, flubs, stubs, hooks, slices, shanks, and other lapses from perfection. Of course, I never fully succeed, but I do know how to bogie.

A bogie is one over par, not terribly satisfying, but

obviously better than two, three, four, or more over par. Keeping score is easy with the bogie–measure: even bogies, one over, two over, one under, two under. Four over keeps me under 50 for nine. Five under calls for a shift to the par–measure—one more par and I break 40, unless it's accompanied by a double bogie (or worse).

There are so many ways to bogie—landing behind trees or in sand traps, hitting short of the green, over the green, left or right, three putting.... It's so easy, and so natural. And good-natured amateurs shouldn't really care. It's just a game. Besides, I'm told, I look pretty good even when I bogie. I *look* like I know what I'm doing, even if I don't. And there are *so* many others who do much worse.

So what's different about dancing? As an eighth grader, I *knew* I could dance. My brother Peter saw me the first time I got on the dance floor. The very next day, in my presence, he expressed his astonishment to my parents: "I couldn't believe my eyes. There's my little brother out there *dancing*. I'm a senior and still don't know what I'm doing. He just walked right out there like he's been doing it all his life!" I'm just a *natural*, I thought to myself.

But in the ninth grade I made the mistake of dancing with that little red-headed girl, Annie Painter. After a few times around the floor, she smiled politely and offered some advice, "Not bad, but I wish you wouldn't just go around and around in circles." A little bit of self-consciousness began to displace my self-confidence. Still, a few squares, triangles, oblate spheroids, and a rhombus or two would fix everything.

Unfortunately, there was little time for that. Mid-year we moved from Traverse City to Milford. Traverse City had its own high school dance band, which specialized in pieces by Glenn Miller, the Dorsey Brothers, and the like. Milford played records, straight from Dick Clark's, "Hit Parade." Unfamiliar music and unfamiliar dancing and, of course, unfamiliar kids.

Still, I'd moved and adjusted many times before. I learned cursive in kindergarten in a one-room schoolhouse in Sharon Valley. We moved to Bay City the next year. My new first-grade classmates in the two-room schoolhouse wondered what on earth I was doing when we were asked to write our names, but I quickly learned to print just like they did. So, why couldn't I learn how to dance Milford-style?

Well, I did, more or less, but somewhere along the line one of my dance partners commented that I had an "interesting" way of dancing. "How so?" I innocently asked. "Well, you don't exactly dance to the beat. It's kind of, like, the off-beat. But it's still nice." The *off-beat*, what's that? I wondered.

Then I recalled something my mother said when I first started dancing: "Dancing is so easy. Anybody can do it. But what I can't *stand* is when somebody can't dance to the beat." Dance to the beat? What does that mean? I wondered, but didn't bother to ask. It reminded me of a remark she made about Bay City Handy's high school marching band just before we moved to Traverse

City. "Just look at them," she said, "Half of them are out of step." I knew this was meant as a criticism, but their feet moved so fast that I couldn't really see what she meant. So how important could it be?

Not at all, coming from my mother, I thought. But coming from my dance partner was something else again, and if she thought I danced to the off-beat, or whatever, there must be others who think so, too! Dancing is supposed to be so *easy*. Not dancing to the beat is so *awful*. Apparently I didn't get it, and I wasn't about to make it worse by *asking* someone for help.

The only solution was to *think* my way through this. Watch others move their feet, listen to the music, and put two and two together. But, just like the marching band, everything moves so quickly and in so many directions. Everyone seems to be dancing differently, but they all must have it *right*—except for me.

The golf lesson should be obvious. *Thinking* my way through the golf swing is not nearly as effective as *feeling* my way through it. Thinking too much causes failure. *Feeling* my way through the swing is necessary, even if it doesn't always work well and even if it never works to perfection. Worrying about what others think my swing looks like never helps. People's golf swings are very different. There are many ways to hit a ball and many more than one that produce good results. Golf can be fun despite one's shortcomings—sometimes even because of them. Golf can be frustrating, but it can also be very amusing. Not everyone can play the game well, but nearly everyone can enjoy themselves at it.

Okay, the golf lesson *is* obvious. Now my only recourse is the adage, "You can't teach an old dog new tricks." Of course, that's probably false. Every once in a while Millie catches me moving my feet around as if I might give in. A couple of years ago she commented, "Maybe once you're an old man you'll lose your self-consciousness and end up dancing after all."

Maybe I will, but not just yet. I may know to bogie, but where's the beat in the boogie?

Milford

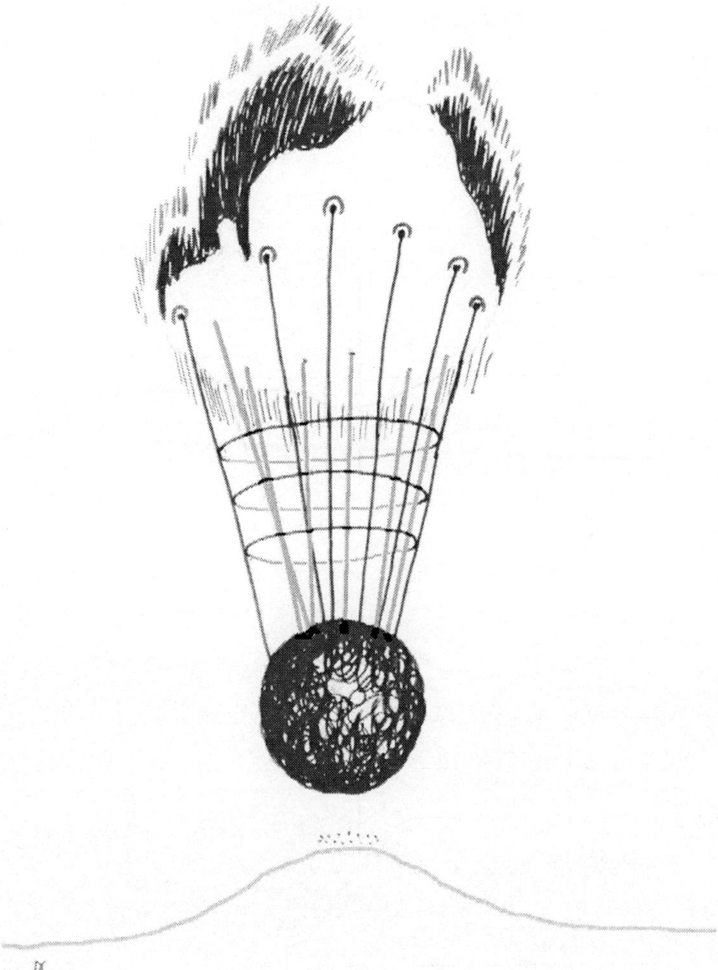

Moving to Milford

Midway through my first year in high school we moved from Traverse City to a knotty-pine house nestled in the woods, four miles from Milford. Once owned by my father's older sister, Besse, it was now abandoned.

Aunt Besse had sold her home and moved to Plymouth, where she taught school. The knotty-pine house was on a plot of land adjacent to where she had lived. Built by her son Glenn, it was financed by the teachers' union to which she belonged. She told my father that she was turning the house over to the teachers' union, which thus far had shown little interest in the property. Since the legal process was moving along very slowly, she saw no reason why we couldn't live there in the meantime.

We moved into our new, rent-free home in late January. The only problem was that the steam radiators were lying in the snow outside the house. Since Aunt Besse had no further use for the house, Glenn never installed the radiators. That task would be ours. My father and I dug up a couple of the smaller ones and brought them into the house. The larger ones would wait until my brother could make the 25-mile trip from Ann Arbor to help carry them in. Then, of course, my father had to figure out how to connect them and make the entire system work. Meanwhile, we tried to keep ourselves warm in the sub-zero weather by huddling around the two fireplaces.

It took more than a week before we were settled in enough for my parents to take me into Milford to enroll in the high school. It was the middle of a six-week marking period, and I was put into classes which seemed closest to those I'd been taking in Traverse City. Lost in the shuffle was Biology.

All the Milford freshmen took Biology, whereas it was a sophomore class in Traverse City. The opposite was the case with Latin, so I ended up with a bunch of sophomores in Latin, and I never did take a high school Biology class.

I had a lot of adjusting to do, seemingly in mid-stream—not the least of which was figuring out who might be my new friends. We had moved many times before; this was my eighth new school and making new friends was something I'd gotten used to. But this time was the hardest. I loved Traverse City, and I thought I would never again have friends like those I'd left behind.

My only consolation was that Milford was a smaller school and, presumably, I'd have a better chance making the basketball team next year. I had already suffered the heartbreak of not making the freshman team in Traverse City, while several of my friends had. My pal Fritz Drulliard was already over 6' tall and clearly was the varsity's center of the future. Gary Murner was even shorter than I was, and he'd never distinguished himself in our back-alley basketball games. Yet, there he was, starting at guard! Bruce Eckhardt didn't have a jump shot, and was easy to block in alley ball. Why couldn't I at least have been given a seat next to him on the bench?

When I told Fritz we were moving, he predicted I'd be a basketball star in little Milford, a village of fewer than 2,000 people. Fritz wore glasses with thick, case-hardened lenses when playing basketball. That's what I should do next year.

No wonder I didn't make the freshman team: I was the youngest kid in my class, short, and blind as a bat without my glasses! Next year, I'd still be the youngest kid in my class, but I'd get some hardened glasses, and maybe I'd be at least a little taller than 5' 4 ½".

The clincher was that I had Pinky Witt's outdoor backboard. Pinky was the leading scorer on Traverse City High School's varsity basketball team and one of my brother Peter's best friends.. His back-alley court was just a block down the street from ours. Pinky, Peter, and their pals spent long summer hours playing alley ball at Pinky's. Now they had all gone off to college, with Pinky bequeathing his backboard to me.

My optimism was short-lived. It turned out that Milford High School wasn't so small, after all. It was a consolidated school, drawing students from as far as 15 miles away. In fact, when we moved to Milford, the basketball team was ranked third in the state in Class B, and most of the players were juniors. The freshman and junior varsity teams were outstanding as well.

However, I had until the next November to figure out how to make the junior varsity basketball team. Meanwhile, I could check out my chances of making the golf team, and soon discovered that they weren't high. Sure, I'd *once* shot 59 for nine holes in Traverse City, but Ed Tokarski, also a Milford freshman, was already shooting par and Pete Lodge, another freshman, wasn't far behind.

It was clear that I wasn't going to get to play in any of the matches. So, for the first match of the year, I asked if I could caddy for fourth man, Dennis Barry. Coach Richard Yeager agreed. Just before Dennis was scheduled to tee off, I asked him if I could take a practice swing with his driver. Apparently we both underestimated how flat my swing was—I struck his hand on my backswing. Nevertheless, Dennis played the match, aching hand wrapped in a towel in between shots. Having won the coach's disfavor so easily, I didn't have the nerve to ask him if I could substitute for Dennis.

In fact, Dennis's hand was broken, and he didn't play in any further matches. I neither caddied again nor played in any matches. But I did practice with the team, and my game quickly improved. I began regularly to score in the low 50s, and occasionally in the high 40s. One day I reported shooting a 45. At this point two of the seniors took me aside to tell me that I'd better not turn in any more scores like that. No way should a little freshman like me threaten to replace a senior in the lineup. During this little "lecture," one of the seniors pulled out a jackknife, opened it, and began moving it slowly back and forth a few inches from me. I could feel my face pale and my stomach churn.

After practice Coach Yeager gave me a ride back to Milford. Noticing that I was unusually quiet, he asked me if something was wrong. I immediately broke into tears. Reluctant to be a tattletale, yet frightened for my life, I eventually told him what had happened. Coach told me he'd take care of the problem, and he encouraged me to keep working hard on my game, someday it would pay off.

That was the last time the young man with the knife played golf for Milford High School. Although Coach Yeager told me that I needn't worry about him bothering me again, I spent the rest of the school year carefully keeping my distance. But next year the bully would be gone, I'd be back, and so would Coach Yeager.

Coach Yeager

Mr. Richard Yeager was my golf coach for four years at Milford High School. He was also the head football coach. I'd heard that Coach Yeager had a fiery temper and intemperate tongue on the football field, but I'd never seen that side of him. I knew him as a firm but soft-spoken mentor on the golf course.

Still, I wasn't tempted to play football until the summer before my senior year at Milford. After several spurts of growth the past three years, I was now over 6' tall and weighed nearly 160 pounds. I'm big and strong enough, I thought.

"Why *not* go out for football?" I asked myself while mowing the grass at Hickory Hill Golf Course. Coach Yeager seldom played at Hickory Hill Golf Course, but I looked up and there he was. Why not tell him what I'm thinking?

"Why would you want to do *that*, Michael?" he asked.

"Because I need to get in shape for basketball, and I really don't like cross-country running," I replied.

"What makes you think you'd like football?" he rejoined.

Recalling my junior high days of ineptitude on the gridiron, I was hard–pressed to come up with a plausible answer. "Maybe I could be a wide receiver," I offered.

"Without your glasses, Michael? You have to see the ball to catch it, you know."

"Maybe I could play on the line without glasses, Coach."

Conceding that I was bigger and stronger, Coach Yeager pointed out that I had no experience and it was quite likely that I wouldn't get much playing time in games. It didn't look like a very promising choice, he said. If my main objective was to get in shape for basketball, he added, cross country was the ideal sport.

As usual, Coach Yeager was right. But, maybe he shuddered at the thought of having to deal with me on the gridiron as well as the golf course. After all, I was the same kid who nearly wiped out his trunk full of Spalding Air Flite golf balls every spring. "Michael, how could you have already lost all the balls I gave you just the other day?" he'd ask. I was also the same kid who delayed the golf team's departure for a match by accidentally dropping my wallet in the toilet. And if I wouldn't take his advice to slow down my swing or to aim left of the pond instead of trying to go over it, how could I be counted on to stick to the football plays?

Still, it seemed that Coach liked me. He always gave me a ride from school to the golf course and then back to Milford. Sometimes he gave me a ride all the way home, four miles beyond Milford. Aware of the absence of my father and financial difficulties at home, he frequently asked how things were going for me beyond the classroom and golf course.

In the spring of my senior year Coach Yeager asked who I was taking to the senior prom. "No one," I said. "I'm not asking anyone to the prom."

"I think you're making a mistake, Michael," he advised. "You may find it hard to realize this now, but later you'll look back and regret not having gone to your senior prom."

"I didn't get a class ring either, Coach," I replied. "I decided I couldn't afford one. Besides, once I'm out of high school, when would I wear it? Same thing about the prom. It costs a lot of money, and I don't even have a girlfriend right now. So what's the point?"

"It's part of the high school experience. You'll be missing something that someday you'll wish you hadn't." Well, Coach Yeager was wise and usually on target, but maybe he missed the mark on this one. More than 45 years later, I still have no regrets about not going to the prom. In fact, I've never even been to a class reunion. Still, I do remember Coach's advice. What will I talk about if there's a fiftieth reunion and someone convinces me to show up?

Summer Work

Before high school I thought summer vacations were supposed to be just that—*vacations*, time for fun and play. Our family's slim, rather unpredictable financial resources and my growing realization that *fun* didn't always mean *free* changed my perspective. Summer vacations were for working. One year of high school behind me, I was fourteen and needed a job.

My first opportunity was caddying at Orchard Lake Country Club. One Saturday Hughie Heintzelman and I hitchhiked 15 miles down several different roads, only to spend half the day waiting for a chance to carry someone's bag, while making sure we'd be finished in time to hitchhike back home before dark. During the wait, Hughie invited the other caddies to test my grip. "Shake hands with this guy," he'd say. "He's got some kind of grip."

Indeed, I had inherited my father's strong grip, and I was happy to display it. I figured that if the other caddies knew I had strong hands, they might think that I could more than hold my own if anyone cared to start a fight. Luckily, no one called my bluff. Hughie and I decided not to return to Orchard Lake Country Club.

Soon a second opportunity came my way. I learned through my classmate Tom Hubbell that the Detroit Gun Club, just a few miles away, was looking for weekend workers. The hours would be long, but the pay predictable. The Detroit Gun Club, it seemed to me, was a weekend haven for wealthy shotgun specialists who didn't mind driving out in the country to fire away at clay pigeons hurling through space. They called it skeet shooting. My job was to release those spinning pigeons at the simple command, "Pull!" Any delay in pressing the button evoked visible irritation and often drew verbal abuse from the shooters.

I preferred working in the pits below ground level and out of view of the shooters. My task was to place clay pigeons, one at a time, on the continually moving armature that hurled the circular disks in a variety of directions away from the shooters. Occasionally a cracked clay pigeon would break into several pieces after leaving the pit. Out of view of the shooters, I could smile with impunity. At the end of the day we had to pick up all the shotgun shells the shooters left lying at their feet. Basically the work was noisy, dirty, and boring. Little fun and little money. Next summer, I thought, I'll have to find a better job—quieter, cleaner, more fun, and much more money.

One afternoon my brother Peter and I decided to play a round of golf at a little golf course we'd discovered only a few miles down the road, Hickory Hill Golf Course. As we surveyed the sixth hole, with one pond directly in front of the tee and a second one just beyond it, a young man was just finishing trimming grass around the tee. I knew I'd never be able to drive straight over the two ponds toward the green. But noting that the hole was only 320 yards long, Peter was wondering how far he'd have to carry the ball in order to make it over the second pond so he asked the young man.

A friendly conversation followed, and eventually we asked him about his job on the golf course. He replied that he'd cut grass, raked sand traps, and done odd jobs on the course for the past three summers—good pay and all the golf he wanted to play. "Wow, that's the kind of job I'd like to have," I later said to Peter, thinking at the same time that I could never be so lucky.

Well, I was wrong. Although my father was seldom around during the Milford years, apparently he did frequent Henderson's countryside bar. There he met "Old Mac," owner of nearby Hickory Hill Golf Course. Old Mac mentioned that the young man who had worked for him the past several summers was graduating from high school and wouldn't be coming back next summer. At my father's urging, I applied for the job and, to my surprise, Old Mac hired me. Forty hours a week at a dollar an hour and, best of all, free golf! Money and fun—a very good deal for a fifteen-year old in 1956.

For the next two summers I worked from 7:00 A.M. to mid-afternoon during the week and played golf until nearly dark. I learned to fertilize greens, run water sprinklers, run a power mower, rake sand traps, lay sod, and drive a pick-up truck before I had a driver's license.

On Saturday and Sunday mornings I arrived at the first hint of daybreak to rake the traps, whip the morning dew off the greens with a long bamboo pole, and emptied waste baskets on the tees. I finished just as the rush of weekend golfers arrived, and I often returned to play later in the day, after the crowd of golfers thinned.

Best of all, after two summers at Hickory Hill, my incurable slice was replaced by a sometimes controllable hook!

Leon's Lessons

"Hey, kid," Leon called out, "drive the truck over here."

"But I don't know how to drive!" I replied.

"You can do it. Push in the clutch, turn on the key, then ease out the clutch. Just make sure it's in first. You've seen me do it a hundred times."

"But I don't have a license. I just turned fifteen, remember?"

"Jeemis Crimis, I've been driving since I was twelve. You only need to drive it 30 yards over to here." Although Leon certainly was not averse to swearing, he insisted he never took "the Lord's name in vain." He'd had enough bad luck without inviting even more. Now in a second marriage, he frequently complained about the judge "garnishing" his wages.

As head groundskeeper at Hickory Hill Golf Course, Leon was my summer mentor. I learned a lot from him. When I told him I'd never heard the word "garnishing" before, he taught me another, "allmy-money." Both these words came in handy a short time later when my mother told me my father's wages were being "garnisheed" because of his failure to pay alimony and child support.

Now he was offering me a driving lesson, from a distance. Aside from Leon himself, the only thing within 30 yards of the beat-up, old pickup was a sand trap. If things got out of control, I could always aim for it. This was my big chance. Some of my classmates were already driving family cars on dates, but had they ever driven a pickup on a golf course—when they were only fifteen?

I eased the clutch in, turned the key, popped out the clutch, and lurched halfway to Leon. Jamming on the brakes, but ignoring the clutch, I brought the pickup to an abrupt stop, killing the engine. "Not bad, kid," observed Leon. "Looks like you could stop on a dime."

In almost no time at all I mastered both clutch and brake. Soon I was driving all over the course, in circles, forward, backward, even in and out of the old equipment shed that afforded just a foot clearance on either side. To convince all onlookers that I was man enough for the job, I cultivated a frown and pressed my left arm down hard on the window frame to make it look like I actually had biceps on my 6', 138-pound frame.

I should have learned my lesson about such deceptions a few years earlier. Trying to keep my arms permanently flexed one day in the seventh grade, I heard Bethel Jean shout across the classroom, "Don't play with them, Mike—they'll grow!" Shortly after this embarrassing moment, I moved to another school.

When I next saw Bethel Jean, we were college freshmen. She immediately reminded me of my feeble flexings. She also reminded me of my moniker, "The Limburger Kid," which I earned by stuffing Limburger cheese sandwiches in my locker each morning and then brandishing them around the lunchroom several hours later. Like my grandfather L.H. Eddy, I knew a tasty sandwich when I smelled one, even if it came at the expense lunchroom companionship.

But I had come a long way since the seventh grade. Eleventh grader-to-be, I could handle any driving challenge on the golf course until the day the new pickup arrived. Leon always arrived at work before I did. On this particular day, so did his boss, Old Mac, owner of Hickory Hill. Old Mac usually confined himself to the clubhouse. As far as I knew, he had never seen me driving the old pickup, and he knew I wasn't old enough to have a driver's license. So I froze when Leon said, "Back out the new truck, kid."

"It's okay, kid," said Old Mac. "Leon tells me you're a good driver. Come on, back it out."

Eyeing the row of vertical supports only a few inches from driver's side of the shiny new pickup, I gulped deeply and muttered, "I don't think I can do it."

"Sure you can, kid," insisted Old Mac. "This pickup's only a little bit wider than the old one. Here, take the keys."

Inching the truck backward I heard a sound very much like a new piece of chalk scraping the wrong way against the chalkboard. The three of us surveyed the deep, long crease on the side of the pickup. Trembling, I prepared myself for the worst.

"That's all right, kid," comforted Old Mac. "Now it's broken in. That sort of thing's bound to happen out here sooner or later." With that, Old Mac sauntered back to the clubhouse, leaving Leon and me to begin our work for the day.

"There's a lesson in this, kid," said Leon. "Even good drivers have accidents. Try to be careful, but that's not always enough. Jeemis Crimis, it ain't your fault. I might've done it myself."

A year and half later I was hoping my mother would be similarly understanding. My parents' divorce was now final, and my mother was scheduled to begin a new job the next day. Meanwhile, the roads were icy as I set out for home from the school dance. Cruising up the last hill before reaching home, I went into a skid at 40 mph. This was the time to apply Driver Education Cardinal Skidding Rule No. 1: Do *not* apply brakes when going into a skid. I thought of this just after hitting the brakes.

The car slid into a large ditch, spun completely around and flipped over, leveling the top of our Studebaker convertible. Had I gone into my skid only a few feet later I would have wrapped the car around the base of a thick, very sturdy, state park sign. Miraculously, I escaped with a only a few scratches.

Fortunately, friends driving a short distance behind me stopped and took me the rest of way home. Having witnessed the accident, they were sure they would find me crushed to death. Instead they were quite

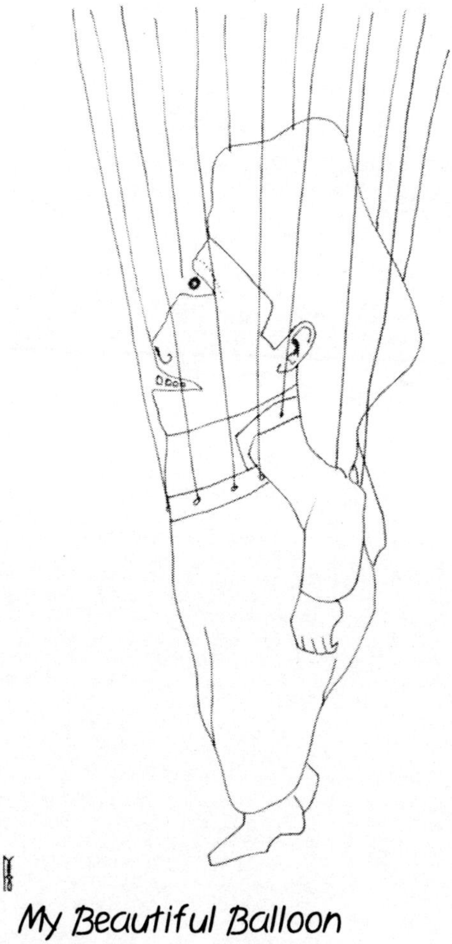

My Beautiful Balloon

surprised to see me standing beside the car, mumbling that I probably should turn off the car radio.

I awakened my mother with the announcement that I'd had "a little accident." Emerging from deep sleep and seeing me hovering over her bed, apparently unharmed, she groaned, "Just how am I supposed to get to my new job tomorrow?" But, shocked to see how badly crushed the car was, she wondered how I could have survived, let alone walked away nearly unscathed. So did I.

The car was put on display at one of the local gas stations for the next week, and its picture made the front page of the weekly Milford paper. Overhearing someone say, "Well, nobody got out of that one alive," I pointed out that I was the driver, fortunately with no passengers. Somehow, as the car flipped, I must have flattened myself against the front seat, thus avoiding any contact with the collapsing roof.

For the next several days I felt somewhat dazed as I ran up and down the basketball floor in practice—almost as if I were floating outside my body. Leon's lessons hadn't prepared me for this.

The Furies

According to my *American Heritage Dictionary*, "*Furies* (fyoor'ez) *pl.n. Gk. & Rom. Myth.* The three terrible, winged goddesses who punish doers of unavenged crimes."

I don't know if they are goddesses, gods, spirits, or whatever. Maybe they originate from ancient Greece or Rome, but their presence was evident on every golf course I saw in the 1950s. Far from mythical, they seemed to reside in virtually all young male golfers of my acquaintance.

Here's how they worked. Young male golfer X would commit the crime of defaming, defacing, or despoiling the innocent. He might curse the wind, hurl his golf club, or tear up the turf. Incapable of framing evil intent or even the desire for retaliation, how could the wind be anything but an innocent victim of an unavenged crime? The same, of course, was true of X's pliant golf club, not to speak of the nearby turf lying there minding its own business.

Noticing this, little Furies would go to work on young male golfer X. They might make even viler obscenities spew uncontrollably from his mouth. Or they might cause a paroxysmal coiling of his entire body from which he could be relieved only by hurling his club to the skies or by tearing up more turf.

Of course, such vengeance was wrought at the expense of even more defaming, defacing, or despoiling of the innocent, but since it was kind of a double vengeance, it was worth it. The Furies' work would destroy X's concentration and ruin his game for at least the next three holes. In addition, since the Furies were invisible, they made X look like a fool to all onlookers.

Actually, the Furies were doubly invisible—and this made their vengeance all the more thorough. Onlookers could not see them avenging the innocent. They could see only an apparent fool. But the Furies were also invisible to the apparent fool. This meant that, in addition to *looking* like a fool, often young male golfer X *felt* like a fool after the Furies left.

Still, this wasn't the worst of it. Sometimes the Furies were doubly devious, too. Here's what I mean. Home from college for a few days, my brother Peter thought he'd show me he could drive the 320-yard sixth hole at Hickory Hill Golf Course. All that stood between him and the green were two ponds. As soon as he hit a 200-yard duck hook into the second pond, he defamed his driver.

Being a young male golfer myself at the time, I didn't recognize the symptoms. But now I realize that the red rush in his neck was a sign that the Furies were about to go to work. Peter's next drive dribbled into the first pond, 50 yards off the tee. His third and fourth drives followed suit.

The Furies were fearsome that day. Peter teed up a fifth ball, whirled around, and stalked in my direction. I quickly swallowed my smirk and I stepped aside. He took three giant strides to the back of the tee, screamed curses at the gods, and pivoted 180 degrees. By the time he had taken his second stride back toward the ball, his driver was fully coiled for the kill. Seconds later I watched his ball land on the back of the green of that 320-yard hole. It was the hardest, most terrifying swing I'd ever seen. Peter then two putted for the most spectacular 11 I'd ever seen.

No doubt Peter's momentary triumph simply gave the Furies more opportunities to work on us. I was still trying to duplicate his feat two years later. But that was the summer I finally decided not to throw clubs anymore.

For three years I had two hand-me-down woods in my bag. Even my father and brother acknowledged that the driver was a challenge. I stayed with the 4-wood. But now that I had finally figured out how to stop slicing my drives, I decided it was time to buy my own set of woods. Old Mac, my boss at Hickory Hill, offered me a deal—a set of four persimmon woods for $40, the equivalent of one week's wages. So, I was going to take special care of those persimmon woods.

Unfortunately, the Furies always seemed to be waiting for me on Hickory Hill's fourth hole. On the fateful day, my second shot was so poor that I didn't even watch it come to a stop. I was ten yards beyond it before I realized I had walked too far. I took out an iron, set down my bag, and went back to hit my third shot. It was fat city, and I was furious. Eyes shut, I hurled my iron. I opened them just in time to see my club bounce off my golf bag. Inside my bag was my newly purchased 2-wood, with its newly severed shaft.

I hid my broken 2-wood in the attic, hoping that no one would notice I was carrying one fewer club in my bag. I vowed never again to throw a club. Instead I permitted myself to swing it as wildly and furiously as I wished after hitting a lousy shot, as long as I didn't let go.

And I didn't let go—not even when I snapped off the head of my 3-iron while punching a hole in the bottom of my golf bag. I buried the broken club in a ditch and made the hole in my bag as inconspicuous as I could.

It shouldn't have taken so long for me to figure out the vengeful Furies' ways. It was there for all to see in the ninth grade. A player on an opposing team treated everyone on the course to a two-hour temper tantrum. It culminated on the last hole as it began to rain. He hit his first drive into the pond. Then the Furies took over.

We watched in disbelief as his driver slipped from his hands on his second try. It soared high in the air and splashed down in the middle of the pond. It's the only time I've ever watched someone fish for a golf club from a rowboat. My guess is that the club is still there. The Furies exacted a heavy toll from that young male golfer.

It took several years of punishment before the Furies decided I had learned their lesson. They seldom visited me after I buried my 3-iron. My game improved, never to the point of excellence, but occasionally to my satisfaction.

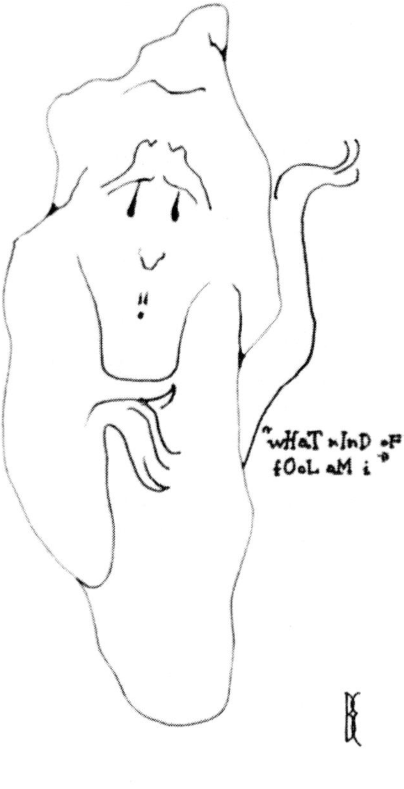

Growing Pains

I couldn't imagine a better sport than basketball. Dribble, spin, shoot, jump, run.... That was the problem, you had to run, run, run.... Golf was fun and certainly challenging. But no matter how many holes I played during the long summer months, golf couldn't prepare me to run up and down the basketball floor. How about football in the fall? Maybe that would get me in shape. I had grown quite a lot since playing on the eighth grade team in Traverse City: from 5' 4" then, to 5' 5" when I moved to Milford in the middle of the ninth grade, 5' 10" in the tenth, and now a full 6' going into the eleventh. Unfortunately, most of my growing was upward; I was skinny as a rail.

Still, the shadow of my brother lingered. He had said he was skinny too (even though he wasn't *that* skinny), but he had played football. Maybe he was away at college, but once in a while I had to tell him what I was (or wasn't) doing. Somehow I had survived his imagined tauntings in the tenth grade. How could I survive a second year? How about my glasses? I needed them to see, but they wouldn't be protected under a football helmet. "Take 'em off, chicken," I could imagine my brother saying. "What's to *see*, anyway? You just *hit*." And *get hit*, I worried.

There had to be something I could do save face. Gerry Flynn came to my rescue. He suggested I join him on the cross-country team. "I've never done anything like that before," I replied.

"That's okay. Mr. Gabier's the coach—a great runner in college. He knows all about getting in shape." The first day of practice convinced me of that. Coach Gabier led us in warm-ups. Deep-knee bends were important, he stressed. As he squatted down, I noticed muscles popping out beside his knees. Glancing down at my bent knees, all I could see was skin and bone. Where did all *those* muscles come from?

As we began running that fall, Coach Gabier commented that I had good running form. All I had to do was gradually build up my pace. Easier said than done. I faced several obstacles. First, although all the other runners lost weight as they rounded into shape, I gained 20 pounds! Second, I had a problem with pain. I didn't like the side aches that inevitably set in during races. Gerry told me not to worry about it. His tactic was to run through the pain. The trick, he said, was to keep running until you vomit; then the pain would go away. Third, I had an intense aversion to vomiting, and I took every caution not to cross that threshold. Fourth, I was determined always to save enough strength to finish the race. Unfortunately, I never figured out how much was just the right amount to hold in reserve; my last quarter mile was always considerably faster than my first.

Undistinguished as my running was, it did enable me to run circles around the football players during the first week of basketball practice. However, once the games started, a few weeks on the bench removed whatever advantage I may have had. Still, I had found an answer for my brother, and there would be next year!

The fall of my senior year brought a couple of surprises. My buddy Tom Hubbell came back to school with big muscles and speed after a summer of lifting weights and running in combat boots. "Big T" had been as familiar with the bench in football as I was in basketball. Suddenly he was a star, tackling people left and right; by the end of the season he was All-League. Maybe there was some hope for me in basketball—only I hadn't worn combat boots playing golf that summer, and it was hard to run around the golf course with a golf bag on my back.

Still, there was cross-country running to prepare for basketball. Once again Coach Gabier had us step on the scales. I matched the 158 pounds I had weighed at the end of the previous season. However, I was nearly two inches taller. Once again, Coach Gabier told me my running form was good, and I was stronger and faster than the previous year. After all, I'd been getting used to my 158-pound body for nine months.

In our first race I "placed." This meant that my time would count in determining which team won. In the previous year I was so far back in the pack that my times never counted in the team scoring. The same thing might have happened in this race if Tom Manley hadn't fallen down. As Tom and I were beginning our final sprint to the finish line, he tripped. A few runners went by us as I bent over to try to help him up. He slapped my hand away and shouted, “Keep going!” I took off and finished just in time to take our last scoring spot.

However, my first “placing” was my last. Once again I was the only weight gainer, this time ten pounds. And I was as dedicated as before that I would not run hard enough to vomit and that I would save enough to finish strong. This beatable combination kept me well behind the leaders. Still, at nearly 6' 2" and now 168 pounds, I was ready for basketball.

Someday?

Usually I had to wait in the school parking lot for my mother to pick me up after basketball practice. However, this time she arrived early, and she came into the gym on that cold January evening. I noticed she was having a conversation with Mr. Richard Yeager, my golf coach. So, there they were, my two sternest critics. What, I wondered, were they saying about my basketball skills.

"What were you and Coach Yeager talking about at practice?" I asked.

"He said that someday you'll be a good golfer," she replied. "But maybe not for a few more years."

"What did he say about my *basketball* playing?" Yearning for some words of encouragement in this, my senior year on the hardcourt, I was disappointed to learn that they hadn't discussed basketball at all. "So what?" I grumbled to myself. "He just coaches football and golf. Besides, he's too short to know anything about basketball."

Only later did Coach Yeager's comment about my golfing potential sink in. Meanwhile, I was wallowing in self-pity. Here I was, a sixteen-year old senior, riding the pine with Willie MacMahon again. Willie and I shared the fate of being the youngest seniors on the team, both of us having started school at the tender age of four. We sat together at the end of the bench as sophomores on Coach Russell Gabier's junior varsity team. As juniors we sat in the same spots on the varsity bench. But now we were seniors, and everything was going to be different. We had finally caught up with our bodies. I had gone from being 5' 10" and 125 pounds as a sophomore to nearly 6' 2" and 168 pounds as a senior. So, I was ready to play ball!

Coach Jack Minzy thought so too, at least for a while. He stopped our intra-squad scrimmage just before the first game and announced in a loud voice, "It's going to be another *long* season if you guys don't shape up! You know, if I had to decide right now on one player to start in the first game, it'd be a guy who's been sitting on the end of the bench for two years. Pritchard's been running circles around all of you—except for Willie, who sat right beside him. Those guys *want* to play—and they deserve to. I don't know what to say about the rest of you, other than that you're a pathetic excuse for a basketball team!"

Milford High School had been the scourge of the Wayne–Oakland County League during the mid-1950s, averaging over 80 points a game, until Willie and I came along. Suddenly Coach Minzy had to deal with a bunch of losers.

We won only two games my junior year. No doubt Coach Minzy had mixed feelings about the "veteran" team returning for my senior year. Only two had graduated from the previous year's crew. And now he was faced with the prospect of starting Pritchard—of all people!—the skinny kid with thick, case-hardened glasses and basketball shoes that had to be taped together so they wouldn't fall apart. Coach had made the desperate move of shaming his players by threatening to invert his bench, dumping Willie and me right into the middle of the floor.

It must have been too much for Coach Minzy. I didn't start after all. Neither did Willie. But we were the first two off the bench, and in the first half! My first shot was a fadeaway jumper from the side. It hit the corner of the backboard and bounced back harmlessly into my hands as I floated out of bounds. Red-faced, I sprinted to the defensive end of the court, trying to ignore the laughter of my friends in the stands. Still, I had broken the ice; I was in the game. I started at forward in the second half, acquitting myself somewhat better, snagging a couple of rebounds and even making a free shot. By the third game I felt I was coming into own. Afterward Coach Minzy told me I'd played very well. Stage fright behind me, I was ready for more.

Unfortunately, we lost those first three games. Suddenly Willie and I found ourselves on the bench again, wondering what we had done wrong. We soon realized that we weren't the only seniors on the bench. All but one of the seniors had joined us. Evidently this was to be a "rebuilding" year. By mid-season Coach

Minzy was starting sophomores. Still, we lost, and lost, and lost....

"Rebuilding" is not an idea that sits well with high school seniors who believe that now it is *their* turn to see some action. "How can the coach think *sophomores* are better than we are?" Willie and I asked each other. How, indeed? So, naturally I was curious to know what Coach Yeager made of our plight. Could he believe that justice was being done? What did he think of my *basketball* skills? Never mind golf. That could wait until spring.

However, as winter wore on, the hopelessness of my high school basketball career became more evident, and my thoughts began to turn to golf. *Someday* I'll be a good golfer, Coach Yeager said? But maybe not for a *few years*? How could he think that? Hadn't I lowered my average at Hickory Hill last summer to 40 shots per nine? "*Someday*," I thought in the dead of winter sitting next to Willie, "will be the spring of my senior year!"

37

It's understandable that Coach Yeager showed little excitement when I told him I averaged 40 strokes per nine at Hickory Hill the summer before my senior year at Milford High School. This was the nine-hole course that paid me a dollar an hour each summer to cut grass, rake sand traps, and do odds and ends—and which, more importantly, allowed me to play golf free after working hours.

"Just remember," Coach Yeager cautioned me, "you played the same course every day. You shouldn't expect to do as well on courses less familiar to you. And don't forget, Duck Lake is our home course, not Hickory Hill; it's a lot more challenging."

Coach Yeager was a smart man. He had played both Duck Lake and Hickory Hill. He also had a good memory. He remembered my telling him during my junior year that I had averaged 42 the previous summer. Unfortunately, he also remembered that as a junior I averaged 47 during our matches.

Doubtless Coach Yeager's enthusiasm for the

coming season was dampened considerably by the ineligibility of Ed Tokarski, a par shooter since his freshman year. Warned many times that D's weren't good enough, Ed would just smile and reassure everyone that he'd make it. Believing he would, I was fully prepared to play third man behind him and Fred Coxen, whose averages had been several strokes below mine for the past two seasons. With my improved game, I thought, a league championship was clearly within reach.

But what would happen now that our star was ineligible? Much to everyone's surprise, my pre-season scores were slightly lower than Fred's. As we were about to begin our first match, Coach Yeager announced that I would be playing "first man." I found myself pitted against Holly High School's best golfer and one of its star basketball players. Only a junior, he was to help lead his basketball team reach the state finals the next year. I was somewhat awestruck as we teed off.

As the match progressed, it dawned on me that something was very different. I wasn't sitting at the end of the bench watching my opponent bring the ball up the floor. I was on my feet, matching him stroke for stroke. Then I edged ahead on the last hole, finishing with a 37, my best score ever.

"This is it," I thought. "*Someday* has arrived!"

Coach Yeager complimented me on a fine round and then gently took me aside. "Michael, you should feel very good about your round, but don't let it go to your head. Everything went right for you today, but this is probably the best score you'll have this year. That's all right. You'll do fine. Just don't set your expectations so high that you press too hard and end up disappointed." I nodded in agreement but said to myself, "We'll see about my not shooting another 37."

I eagerly anticipated the next day in school. Each morning the principal, Mr. Rasmussen, made announcements over the public address system. For the first time in four years everyone would hear *my* name announced. "Yesterday Milford's golf team won its opening match against Holly. Low man for Milford with a 37 was Michael Pritchard [pronounced Pri-CHARD]."

Peels of laughter reverberated off the walls—my great moment shattered by Mr. Rasmussen's loud, clear mispronunciation of my last name. However, I decided I was willing to have my name mispronounced over the PA as many times as I might post the lowest score, especially if I matched my opening 37.

I didn't have to wait long for the opportunity to try to prove that Coach Yeager had underestimated me. Our next match was only four days away. This time I was paired against another basketball star, Bloomfield Hills' Buddy Badger. Buddy was an even better golfer than Ed Tokarski, and he hit the ball higher and farther than anyone I'd ever seen. But after seven holes in a light rain, we were both 2 over par.

"Not bad for a rainy day on another team's course," I thought. "I wonder why I thought Buddy Badger was so great. Here we are tied with only two holes to go, and I can par in for a 38. Maybe this will give Coach Yeager another thought or two!"

At just that moment the rain came down in a torrent. I struggled in with a pair of sixes, ending up with a 42. At the same time, Buddy turned his game up a notch and finished with a pair of birdies for a 36, a quick lesson in humility for me!

Still, I continued to try to match my 37. The closest I could get was 38, until the state regional tournament. This was my third year at the regionals, always played at Burroughs Farms in Brighton. Unlike our other matches, this one was eighteen holes, with the top three teams qualifying for the state finals. We weren't serious contenders the previous two years. But this year we were undefeated in our dual matches and one of the favorites.

My first two visits to Burroughs Farms were terrifying. There were more than 100 players, all huddled around the first tee as the first group went off. My only consolation had been that most of them had already teed off by the time my name was called. Still, I was so nervous both years that I could barely hit the ball on my first drive, each time dribbling the ball about 50 yards off the tee. But it was different this year.

Once we arrived at the course, Coach Yeager quietly informed me that I would be going off in the first foursome! This was my "reward" for having one of the lowest averages in our region. Then he called the team together. "If you each play your game today, we should qualify for the state finals without any difficulty. Relax, take your time, and keep your heads on straight. Now, there are two *very* important things to keep in mind today. First, there's a rule change. When you mark your ball on the green, do *not* put it in your pocket. That's a two-stroke penalty. Each foursome has a coach as a scorekeeper, and you can bet your life that two strokes will be added to your score if you pocket your marked ball. I know you've been able to change balls in our other matches. But not today. *Everyone got that*?!!!"

"Second, don't take chances. We're playing eighteen holes today—lots of time to make up for a bad shot or two. Don't ask for trouble. If you have an unplayable lie, take a two-stroke penalty and forget about it. Don't do anything foolish. *Got it*?!!!"

As I addressed my drive on the first hole, I could feel the more than 100 pairs of eyes staring at me. How was my stance? Was everyone wondering what *I* was doing in the first group? Look at my old hand-me-down clubs—11 shabby, worn-down sticks, while Tecumseh's Paul Lumpkin's fourteen peerless woods and irons glitter in the morning sun. Could I *please* get the ball off the ground this time? I nervously struck at the ball and watched it sail nicely down the middle of the fairway. I landed a 9-iron on the green and took two putts for a par 4. Much relieved and beginning to relax, I headed for the second tee.

"Mr. Pritchard," said the scorer, "you got a 6 on the first hole. You put the ball in your pocket when you marked it on the green." Stunned, I could not recall *what*

I had done after marking my ball. I protested, "But I didn't even have another ball in my pocket. So I couldn't have changed balls. Are you sure I put my ball in my pocket?"

"I'm sure," replied the scorer.

"Coach will kill me!" I thought. "I can't believe this is happening to me." As I struggled to regain my composure, I reminded myself to relax. "Relax," Coach had said. It's only two shots. Forget it. Seventeen holes to go. Somehow I managed to par the next five holes. "Only 2 over after six holes," I thought, "Coach was right; everything's okay."

The seventh hole was a long par 4—long enough that I had not been able to reach the green in two during either of my previous rounds at Burroughs Farms. This time I wasn't sure what to do. My drive was long and down the middle. Although the green was still not in view, I carefully determined the direction and distance. I sent a 5-iron over the hill straight at the green.

Walking toward the green, I realized that, even with the two-stroke penalty on the first hole, a birdie would give me a good chance for a 37. My hopes were quickly dashed when I saw that, not only was my ball not near the hole, it wasn't even on the green. In fact, it had bounded 15 yards over the green and nestled in a pile of leaves under a tree, two feet from a fence. I stared at my ball in disbelief, "A drive and a 5-iron put me 15 yards over the green. Stymied? Two woods couldn't have gotten me even close until this year."

What should I do? I could take a two-stroke penalty for an unplayable lie. But I already had two penalty strokes. I couldn't swing at the ball from my right side. There's only one other option. Try to chip it out left-handed with the backside of my putter. "Don't take chances," said Coach Yeager. But I had already messed up once. "I *can't* take another penalty." *Whack!* I swung from my left side, but the ball was nowhere to be seen. The backside of my putter had landed behind the ball and buried it in the pile of leaves! Unplayable lie—two more penalty strokes!

I finished the first nine with a 42—37 hits, four penalty strokes, and one whiff. So, I *did* have another 37, in a way. Small consolation, however. We missed qualifying for the state finals by three shots. I could count two of them in my pocket and three more in a pile of leaves. Yes, Coach Yeager was a smart man.

Speaking Up

When I first set foot in Milford High School in mid-January 1955, it was already the middle of one the six-week marking periods. At the end of that period Mrs. Gorseline took me aside and told me that, although she was giving me a C+ in Latin for the marking period, she wasn't sure this was the grade I should get. She said she suspected I could do much better, but so far she had too little evidence of how well I might eventually do.

In the absence of sufficient evidence, I thought to myself, why not postpone giving me a grade until later? But, not inclined to challenge my teachers, I said nothing. Instead, I quietly accepted the burden of trying to explain to my parents why I was the only one of their children to get a C on his report card. Peter's teachers and friends might still be in Traverse City, but his parents were with me in Milford and his shadow still loomed large.

I certainly had ideas about fairness and unfairness during my three and one-half years at Milford High School. But until my last semester I shared them with only one teacher, Mr. Yeager. We didn't talk about fair grading. No, we talked about fairness at a more cosmic level. Mr. Yeager was my golf coach.

We had very different ideas about what I deserved on the golf course. I thought it unfair when my ball came to rest behind a tree. Coach Yeager thought that, by not adjusting for my slice, I got exactly what I deserved.

I thought it unfair when my ball just missed making it over the pond. He thought this was what I deserved for not following his advice and going around the pond rather than trying to hit directly over it.

I thought it unfair that a swing like mine yielded so many awful slices. Coach Yeager thought that, with my wild swing, I was fortunate *ever* to keep the ball in the fairway.

For more than three years we talked about such things. Gradually I came to appreciate his wisdom. As I grew taller, stronger, and more patient, I began to draw the ball rather than slice it. I spent less time in the woods and water. My chips ran closer to the pin, and I had fewer three-putt greens. Best of all, my scores finally began to lower.

However, for me there were endless forms of unfairness to be discovered. Coach Yeager's most important lesson had still to be learned. "Michael," he would say, "golf isn't fair, and it isn't unfair. A lot of it is luck, good luck and bad. You just have to forget your mistakes and misfortunes and keep on trying. Concentrate on one shot at a time. Crying over spilled milk never helps anyone in this game."

Looking back, I marvel at Coach Yeager's patience. It must have been exasperating enough to watch me ignore his advice time and time again. Even worse, he put up with my complaints.

Maybe that's why I was able to talk with him about the B I received on my Government term paper in Mr. Neiner's class. I had worked very hard on the topic of the newly formed European Coal and Steel Community. Receiving a B on that paper dashed my hopes of getting all A's in my last semester of high school. On the way to golf practice I expressed my disappointment to Coach Yeager, complaining that I thought I'd been graded unfairly.

"Michael," he replied, "I think you're very fortunate not to have received an E on that paper. Mr. Neiner mentioned it to me. He was very concerned because it didn't seem to him that it could be entirely your writing."

As Coach Yeager spoke I could feel my face reddening in anger. "You mean he thinks I copied the paper from somewhere?"

"That's right."

"How could he think that?" I asked incredulously. Coach Yeager suggested that, if I really thought I was treated unfairly, I should talk with Mr. Neiner about it.

Another piece of good advice, if only I could muster up the courage. Trembling as I stood before his desk, I addressed Mr. Neiner, "I worked very hard on my paper and thought it deserved a better grade. Can you tell me why you gave it a B?" Mr. Neiner repeated what I had already heard from Coach Yeager, adding that he thought the paper bordered on plagiarism—a very serious matter, indeed.

"If you thought I plagiarized," I replied indignantly, "why didn't you tell me that instead of just giving me a B?" Mr. Neiner replied that he wasn't familiar with my sources, but that the paper certainly didn't look like something written by a high school student.

"But you could have asked me about this. My sister-in-law suggested the topic. She's studying political science at Michigan, and she lent me the main book I used. I'd be happy to ask her to get it for you. Just what, specifically, makes you think I didn't write the paper myself?" Only later did I realize that I was now assuming the role of counter-attacker.

"Look, your paper is full of words that an ordinary high school student doesn't use," Mr. Neiner replied.

"Such as?" I countered.

"Such as 'allocate.' You must have used that word 20 times in the paper. Just what does 'allocate' mean? That's not part of a high school student's vocabulary."

I quickly defined "allocate," pointing out that one

could hardly write about the European Coal and Steel Community without talking about the allocation and re-allocation of resources, since this is what the new community was essentially about. As for a high school student's vocabulary, I added, "Isn't one of the points of writing a term paper to learn new ideas. I didn't know what 'allocate' meant when I started working on my paper, but I had to find out what it meant. Once I did, why *shouldn't* I use the word?"

Mr. Neiner conceded that this is acceptable, but he said that it still seemed to him that the paper was written beyond my level. "What do you know about how I write?" I asked. "I've never written anything for you before. All our tests have been true/false and multiple choice. Did you check with my English teachers about my writing? If you want to know how I write, you should ask Mr. Mathis. I've written a lot for him."

I deliberately omitted mentioning Mrs. Joslin, for whom I had recently written an especially pathetic fictional piece—so pathetic that Mr. Mathis took me aside to express his disappointment that apparently I had joined other students in not taking Mrs. Joslin seriously as a teacher. I had to admit that he was right, and I pledged that I would reform my ways.

At some point Mr. Neiner ended our conversation by taking my paper, crossing out the B, and replacing it with an A. I never knew if I'd convinced him of the merits of my writing, but I felt good about myself. It had been an important moment of self-discovery. Never again would I passively and unquestioningly accept others' assessment of my academic work. So, as I became more acceptant of my fate on the golf course, I began to take charge of myself in the classroom. Not a bad exchange, I thought.

Leaving Hickory Hill

In the spring of my senior year, I worked weekends at Hickory Hill and finally mustered up enough nerve to ask Old Mac for a raise. Since I was planning to go to college the next fall, I could use $1.25 an hour. Besides, I thought, with my experience, I should be worth more. Old Mac told me he'd give it some thought. During the next few weeks I noticed a new face on the grounds, and he seemed to be doing the sort of work that Leon, the head groundskeeper, had done the previous years. Leon was nowhere in sight. I suspected that a big change was afoot. Still, Old Mac said nothing until later that spring when he told me he wouldn't be needing me this year. His younger brother had joined him to run the golf course. Leon was gone, and his brother would handle all the groundskeeping.

Disappointed and feeling somewhat betrayed, I decided I would bring Hickory Hill to its knees with one more round of golf. By now I'd birdied every hole on the course except the dreaded 235-yard par 3 seventh hole. I had eagled five of the nine holes. Of course, this was after playing as many as thirty-six holes a day for the past two summers. I'd never shot better than one over par 36 in a single round. This time, however, I was determined to show who was master.

Not sure that Old Mac would want to give me one last free round, I decided simply to step on the course and play. "I'm entitled to this," I thought. I rode my bike to the edge of the woods by the eighth green, jumped over the fence, and teed off on the ninth hole. I quickly headed off the first tee, hoping either that Old Mac hadn't seen me or that he didn't care.

By the time I reached the seventh hole (once described in the *Detroit Free Press* as the most difficult par 3 hole within 40 miles of Detroit), I was even par. In addition to being very long, this hole had a menacing little tree in the middle of the fairway, just before swooping into a valley, only to rise to an elevated, two-tiered green with large trees and traps on either side of the green. I hooked my drive over the little tree and watched it hit the rise left of the green, kick to the right and stop 30 feet from the pin. Down in two putts, I headed to the eighth tee, still at even par.

More than once I had been undone by the eighth. Despite being straight and relatively flat, its out-of-bounds on the right always seemed inviting, especially when I was having a good round. However, this was to be my last time at Hickory Hill. Before each shot I had said to myself, "This is the last time I'll take a shot from here. Do it right!" My drive went right down the middle. I took out my 8-iron, the most unwieldy of my hand-me-down clubs. It looked more like a thin-faced wedge than an 8-iron, and it was as easy to pop up as to hit a solid shot. "Last time," I muttered angrily. The ball soared toward the green and landed softly three feet from the hole. "Last putt," I shouted with vindictive joy as the ball dropped in the cup for a 34, my first ever sub-par round.

I slung my bag over my shoulder, jumped over the fence, picked up my bike and pedaled down the road—head filled with memories and eyes filled with tears.

Shanking—From Head to Toe

There is no more discouraging shot in golf than the shank. The ball is struck, not on the face of the club, but right where the head of the club joins its shaft. The result is that the shot goes spinning off to the right at a 45-degree angle, never rising more than a few feet off the ground. Typically this is done with short irons: wedges, 9-irons, 8-irons, sometimes even 7-irons. A golfer's first shank of the day is usually totally unexpected; but for the rest of the round, it is feared.

Fortunately, for most golfers, a minor adjustment or two will correct the problem, at least for a while. However, in the summer of 1958 I fell into a shanking swoon. I had just completed my senior season on Milford High School's golf team. I had averaged a shade under 40 shots per nine in our matches, confident that once the summer weather set in, I'd take a couple more shots off my score. Could par shooting be far behind?

However, this would have to be somewhere other than my old stomping ground, Hickory Hill. Old Mac had hired his brother to take care of the grounds; my services were no longer needed. My mother had just begun a full-time job in Pontiac, 20 miles away. Since I was now jobless, she said, we were going to move to Pontiac right away instead of waiting until I went off to college in the fall.

What kind of summer job could I find near Pontiac? How about caddying at the posh Bloomfield Hills Country Club? All I had to do was hitchhike four miles down Telegraph Road and then walk a few hundred yards to the caddyshack. So I gave it a try.

Unfortunately, rich as they were, not many members played very often, and few of those who did were good tippers. Typically I'd arrive at 7:00 A.M. and leave at 4:00 P.M., unless it was my lucky day and I had a late afternoon opportunity. On a really good day, I "double-caddied" (carrying the bags of two players at once) eighteen holes and "single-caddied" an additional nine. On most days, I "single-caddied" nine and sat for hours on the caddy bench, waiting vainly for another chance. By the end of the summer I had saved less than $100 to take with me to college that fall.

However, Monday was "Caddy Day." Caddies could play a free round of golf at the country club. If they were good enough, they could play on the travel caddy team, touring the finest private golf courses in the area and competing with caddies from other clubs. Certain I would make the team, I eagerly looked forward to playing at private clubs with watered fairways, including the fabled Oakland Hills, which had hosted the U.S. Open.

The caddy matches were eighteen holes.

Allowing for good and not so good rounds alike, I told everyone I should shoot somewhere between 75 and 85. Then shanks set in—not just 9-, 8-, and 7-irons, but 6-, 5-, and 4-irons as well. Even my woods spun awkwardly off to the right. I shot over 100 in my first match.

"Don't worry," I told my teammates, "I'll get this straightened out by next week." But I didn't—another 100+ round. The third match was scheduled for Oakland Hills, but I wasn't. Deep in the throes of what I called "summer shanks," I was replaced by another caddy.

For the next several weeks I worked on my swing every evening at home. Where we lived Telegraph Road was separated by a wide, grassy median. I used this as my golf course, hitting whiffle balls up and down the median. Week after week I shanked every club in my bag. I tried my best not to crowd the ball, not to lean forward on my toes, and not to do any of the other things that shankers are known to do.

This was the summer that the song "Volare" was a hit. The tune ran through my head continually. "Volare, volare...Fly, fly...." Fly up, up and away, stupid ball! But it wouldn't.

Meanwhile, I continued caddying. Highlights included: staying away from the caddyshack so that I wouldn't get knifed by the tough Pontiac kid who didn't like me; seeing celebrity Tennessee Ernie Ford as he walked by the caddy bench; caddying for former Secretary of Defense Charles Wilson, who whiffed his 8-iron, taking a ten-inch divot that flew several feet in the air and landed on top of his ball; forecaddying; and becoming the regular caddy of Mrs. Glenn Miller.

Forecaddying was a cooperative venture among caddies. One caddy would go with two players to the tee, while another caddy would carry the two bags ahead about 150 yards in order to get a better view of where the drives ended up. Another part of this practice was an understanding that, when out of full view of the players, the forecaddy would stuff his underwear with golf balls taken from the bags of players reputed to be poor tippers.

The rationale for such theft? I was told, "They're rich, their bags are stuffed with so many balls they'll never miss a few, they're cheapskates who never pay us what we deserve, and every good forecaddy does it—both for himself and the unfortunate guy who has to stay at the tee with those jerks." So, for the first and only time of my life, I became a part-time thief.

Caddying for Mrs. Glenn Miller was a much more positive experience. The first time I caddied for her she asked me for her 5-iron on the tee of a par 3. I gently suggested that, taking the wind into account and the fact that the green was higher than the tee, she might be better off trying her 4-wood. She looked at me and asked, "Are you sure?" I replied that I was pretty sure. She then placed her 4-wood in the middle of the green. When she finished the round, she said to the caddymaster, "I want this young man as my caddy from now on."

During the course of the summer she took time to talk with me between shots about my interests, my family, my college plans, and my own golf game. Mrs. Miller asked me to be her partner during a one-day tournament in which women members at the Bloomfield Hills Country Club paired up with caddies near the end of the summer. I reminded her that I was still struggling with my "summer shanks." "I'm not worried about that," she replied. "I'm sure you'll do just fine."

Well, the organizers of the tournament were sure I wouldn't do just fine. Since I had provided no evidence all summer that I could break 100, they gave me an 18 handicap, apologizing that this was the maximum the tournament rules allowed.

Mrs. Glenn Miller was right. A few days before the tournament, I stopped shanking whiffle balls in the median of Telegraph Road. I didn't know what I did to correct the problem, just that it was now a much more pleasant experience hearing "Volare" running through my head. I told the organizers that I didn't think I should be given an 18 handicap, but they wouldn't hear any such nonsense. So my 80 was converted to 62, and Mrs. Miller and I easily won the tournament.

And I learned a new word, *sandbagger*. "You're just a sandbagger, Pritchard," chided one of the caddies. "You were setting this up all along."

"Sure," I thought, "I went out and deliberately shanked every conceivable shot, missing a chance to play Oakland Hills, just so I could shoot an 80 at the end of the summer and win a member–caddy tournament. Nice act, eh?" But what could I say? They hadn't seen me out there on the median shanking whiffle balls all summer; and even if they had, they might have thought I was just practicing my shanks.

Fifteen years later the "summer shanks" threatened to strike again. This time I noticed something that I hadn't in the summer of 1958. I took my club back slowly, stopped at the top, slowly started my downswing, and saw the toe of the clubhead turned inward by the time it reached the ball. The problem was that I broke my wrists at the top of my swing, not only robbing my swing of power, but also causing me to hit the ball with the *toe* of my club! The shots looked like shanks, but they certainly didn't fit the usual diagnosis. So, it's no wonder the standard remedies didn't work.

Still, since breaking one's wrist at head level causes the ball to behave like a shank, I'm going to call it *shanking—from head to toe*.

Michael *Redux*

The last time I saw Coach Richard Yeager was in the fall of 1967. I had not seen him since graduating from high school in 1958. Newly returned to Michigan from five years in Wisconsin, I was a fresh Ph.D. beginning my first full-time teaching job at Eastern Michigan University. I learned that Coach Yeager ran the pro shop on weekends at the Kensington State Park Golf Course near Milford.

So one fine Saturday morning I suggested to Millie that we take our year-old son, Scott, on a 20-mile drive to meet his daddy's old coach.

Enroute I recalled how I had nearly depleted Coach Yeager's seemingly unlimited supply of shag balls he always carried in the trunk of his car. Spalding Air Flites were his favorites as well as mine. Someday, I thought, I should present him with a box of new Air Flites. As we approached the course, I began to worry. What if Coach wanted to play a round of golf right then and there? Would he still think I swing too hard? *Would* I swing too hard? Would I even be able to get the ball off the ground?

Then a worse fear set in. After nine years, would he even *remember* me? After all, how many students had he had by now? How many football players had he coached? How many golfers?

Holding Scott tightly in my arms, I tentatively stepped into the pro shop. I saw Coach Yeager's familiar form bent over the counter. Engrossed in a newspaper, he didn't look up. I swallowed hard, took a deep breath, and burst out, "Hi, Coach! Remember me?" He raised his head, grinned, and without hesitation replied, "Michael, how could I ever forget *you*?"

I left Eastern Michigan University in 1968, before Coach Yeager had an opportunity to see if I had learned anything about golf in the past ten years. Although I never saw him again, in the ensuing years, I've frequently found him in my dreams.

One recurs even now. I find myself returning to Milford. Although I've completed both my undergraduate and graduate degrees, I discover that I have one more year of athletic eligibility in high school. I wasn't good enough to play in any matches in the ninth grade so I wasn't really on the team. Besides, since I started school at age four, I should have been able to play on the team one more year. Somehow this was overlooked when I graduated at barely seventeen.

I try to remember where Coach Yeager lives. Finally I turn the corner and see him in his yard. "Coach Yeager," I plead, "can I play on the team this year? I just found out I didn't use up all my eligibility. I'd like another shot at the regionals. I won't let you down this time." While waiting for his measured response, I feel a lump forming in my throat—a poignant reminder of those five extra strokes in the 1958 regionals. "Well, I don't know, Michael," he says, "we have a lot of good players now. I'm not sure you can make the team."

As I tee up to see if I really can compete with a bunch of high-school hotshots, I wake up—initially frustrated, but ultimately relieved.

Alma

Arriving at Alma

In the fall of 1958 my brother Peter dropped me off at Alma College, the place where, at age seventeen, I was to begin life on my own—beyond the reach of my mother and someplace where, finally, no one could compare me with my big brother.

I didn't bring much with me. I had $77 in my pocket, the sum total of what remained from my summer earnings as a caddy at the Bloomfield Hills Country Club. For clothes, aside from what I was wearing, I brought a couple of sweaters, a few shirts, a bow tie, an old suit (passed on by my sister-in-law, Penny, courtesy of her deceased father), and a laundry box full of socks, underwear, gym shorts, a couple of pairs of khaki pants, a sweatshirt, a few bathroom necessaries, and a pair of tattered tennis shoes.

For a winter coat, I brought my brother's old Traverse City varsity jacket. This had two advantages over mine. First, it was roomy, whereas I had outgrown my Milford jacket. Second, my brother had removed both his varsity letter and the other sewn on patches that would give away the fact that this was, in fact, a *high school* varsity jacket, whereas telltale inscriptions were woven into the fabric of mine. Peter's jacket did have one serious disadvantage. Its insulation had been ripped out.

I also brought a sawed-off broomstick, a piece of clothesline, an old flatiron, and part of an old scale once used to weigh farm animals. One end of the clothesline was tied around the middle of the broomstick, the other end was attached to the handle of the flatiron. This contraption was used to strengthen my forearms, wrists, and hands by raising and lowering the flatiron. I did this by placing the broomstick in both hands, holding out my arms, and then twisting the broomstick until the flatiron was raised from the floor to the broomhandle and then reversing the process. The scale served as a 35-pound weight whose moving parts clanked against each other with each lift. I might be a skinny 6' 1½", 168-pounder, but I was determined to be a strong one.

Finally, just in case there might be a golf course nearby, I brought my clubs. I transported them in my "Sunday bag," a light, inexpensive, canvas golf bag. Sunday bags were meant to accommodate golfers who wanted to go out and quickly play a few holes without having to lug the more standard bulky bag, complete with large pockets for sweaters, jackets, umbrellas, and who knows what else. Sunday bags had one pocket, with room for only a few golf balls and tees.

It didn't take long to transport this odd array of prized possessions to my room at the far end of the fourth, and top, floor of Wright Hall. As Peter was about to leave, I noticed two young men standing on the corner of Wright Avenue and Main. One stood out because he was so tall, the other because he looked familiar. "Peter," I exclaimed, "isn't that Gordie Snyder from Traverse City?"

"Yeah, it sure looks like him."

"Wasn't he on the golf team with you?" Indeed, Gordie Snyder was on the Traverse City High School golf team. So, just as I was about to take charge of my life, my brother's shadow was already making its entrance. Gordie would recognize my brother's varsity jacket; he probably still had his own. He would remember my brother as first man on the golf team, as a starter on the football team, as an all-A student, and as the popular author of "Pete's Prattles", a weekly column in the high school newspaper. And he'd remember me as Pritch's kid brother.

Gordie introduced us to his fraternity brother, 6' 6" Bert Dugan. So now I knew two students at Alma College. Gordie and Peter talked a few minutes about the good old days in Traverse City. Then I asked the big question, "Does Alma have a golf team?" Yes, he said; and, yes, he was on it. I wondered if I'd be able to make the team and how I'd compare with Gordie Snyder if I did make it—and, indirectly, how I'd compare with my brother.

As my brother departed, I suddenly felt very alone. My roommate still hadn't arrived, and I felt quite uncertain about what lay ahead for me. For the rest of my life, home would be wherever I decided to live, a scary but exciting prospect, and not my parents' decision.

I seldom saw Gordie Snyder after that first day. When the golf season came around, he told me that he was practice teaching and wouldn't have time to play on the team. Not only would there be no comparisons with my big brother, but one fewer player to fight for a spot on the team. Gordie graduated that year, taking my brother's shadow with him. I haven't seen him since 1959.

Bert Dugan and I delivered the campus mail together and, although I've never seen him swing a golf club, we've remained best of friends ever since.

Coach Smith

I met Coach Art Smith on the first day of my freshman classes at Alma College. "This is PE 100," he announced. "We're going to do lots of different things in this class. We'll start with a little boxing. Who'd like to put on these gloves and do a demonstration with Greenie?"

Jim Greenless was also a freshman who had already been on campus a few weeks, practicing on the football team coached by Art Smith. Coach Smith had recruited Greenie and some of the other football players to help out in PE 100. Greenie already had his gloves on. Unfortunately, I happened to be standing right next to Coach. "Here," he said, handing me the other pair of boxing gloves, "you're about the same height as Greenie. And you probably should take off your glasses."

The last time I took off my glasses to engage in fisticuffs I ended up with a bloody nose, courtesy of Art MacCafferty's high school class ring. I never saw his first punch coming. This was in the eleventh grade.

So, I wasn't looking forward to sparing with Greenie, even if it was only a little demonstration.

Coach Smith said we were going to demonstrate how to block a jab. First he had Greenie block my left jab. Then it was my turn. Maybe, I thought, if I try looking in the direction Art MacCafferty's punch came from I'll be able to block Greenie's little punch. Whack! Not realizing Greenie was a lefty, I caught a right jab in the mouth. No bloody nose this time—only a chipped tooth. Greenie apologized profusely, marking the beginning of our friendship; later we played together on the golf team. Even later he became a dentist!

The next spring Coach Smith put out a notice for anyone interested in the golf team to show up at the Pine River Country Club. Noticing my tattered tennis shoes, he asked me where my golf shoes were.

"I don't need any," I replied. "Tennis shoes work just fine for me." I didn't tell him that I couldn't afford golf shoes—just as I couldn't afford shiny, matched clubs like those of my teammates.

"What do you shoot?" he asked.

I paused, wondering what to say. I wasn't quite sure whether my shanking days of the previous summer were completely behind me. "I averaged just under 40 in our high school matches last spring," I answered, "but my game fell apart last summer, so I don't really know."

"Well, you're in the big time now. We play eighteen-hole matches in college. Think you can handle that?"

I certainly hoped so, I replied. That spring was a bit of a struggle, but I started out playing fifth man on the team. Sometimes Coach Smith and the opposing coach joined their fifth men to form a foursome for nine holes. Then the coaches would retreat to the clubhouse so they could greet the other foursomes as they finished their matches. This meant that Coach Smith sometimes had the opportunity to observe my match play rather closely.

On one such Pine River occasion, I started out with fours on each of the first four holes. The fifth hole was a long par 5, shaped like an hourglass with woods on both sides of the fairway.

How would Coach react if I got another 4? First I need a *big* drive right down the middle. I felt my feet slip as I took the club back, causing me to swing even harder than hard, and I watched my ball dribble 100 yards down the left side of the long rough. My second shot was worse, leaving me next to a huge rock, only 175 yards off the tee and more than 300 yards from the green. All hope for another 4 was dashed. But if I could crunch my third shot, pitch up close to the hole, and sink the putt, I could still get a par 5. As I wound up for the kill, feet slipping again, I had one thought too many—don't hit the rock on my follow through. Well, I didn't hit the rock or the ball. It was a clean *whiff*! Three swings later I was on the green, and I two-putted for a triple bogey 8.

As I was readying myself to tee off on the next hole, Coach Smith grinned at me and asked, “Did you whiff one back there, Mike?” I acknowledged that, indeed, I had. “I thought so,” he said, “but I could hardly believe it. I was hoping it was a practice swing. But you were in the rough, and I couldn’t tell from the other side of the fairway.” He commented that he’d never seen anyone whiff a shot in a college match before. “Maybe you’d better think some more about getting some golf shoes. They’d keep your feet on the ground a lot better than those old tennis shoes of yours.” Determined to prove him wrong, I finished the nine with a run of four more 4's, giving me the most unusual 40 I’d ever had.

Noticing that I was still wearing my tattered tennis shoes the next spring, Coach Smith asked me what size shoes I wore. “Ten,” I answered.

“Well, I just happen to have an extra pair of golf shoes that might work for you,” he said, handing them to me. “They don’t quite fit me, so I never wear them. Why don’t you try them on?” They were a perfect fit.

Some 40 years later my old buddy Rich (“Baldie”) Baldwin and Art Smith were reminiscing about the “good old days”. Rich sent me an email saying that Coach recalled that, even though I had a scholarship, I still had to take on a campus job in order to make ends meet. So, he said, when he took a trip to

Florida during the winter break of my sophomore year, he bought me a pair of golf shoes so that I'd be able to keep my feet on the ground!

This was not the only thing Coach Smith bought for me that year. With the aid of those shoes and the new set of irons my brother and mother bought me, I placed fourth in the All-Conference tournament at the Kalamazoo Country Club. Coach was so pleased—and probably surprised—that he bought me a white golf hat with KCC emblazoned on it.

Coach Smith seemed as interested in beating us in golf as coaching us. He probably sensed that we wouldn't listen to him anyway. So he issued a challenge: "I can beat you guys any day using only a 3-iron off the tee. You can hit that long stuff off the tee with your drivers, but all I need is my trusty irons." With that he put his cigar stub between his teeth, tugged on his cap, waggled his 3-iron, and gave us a grin. We suspected that coach teed off with a 3-iron instead of a driver because he couldn't control his woods, but this he would never admit.

In my final season, we came within just a few shots of winning the league championship. For the next decade Coach regularly had championship golf teams, filled with players who regularly shot in the 70s. In fact, our 1962 team was known for some time as the last team *not* to win the championship.

After a few years of teaching at Western Michigan University, I decided to visit Coach while

Kalamazoo College was hosting a match with Alma. Pleased to see me, he introduced me to his team, adding, “Mike played on the team back when nobody could break 80!” I reminded him that every once in a while I did break 80 and that he had even bought me a hat once in celebration of that fact. He then reminded me of my whiff on the fifth hole.

Some 20 years after leaving Alma, I returned for an alumni golf outing. Coach Smith was there. Although I hadn’t played much in recent years, I managed to shoot a 78, making a special point of reporting my score to him. He smiled and said, “Yeah, and I still remember you whiffed the ball on the fifth hole back in ‘59!”

Rolling Green Revisited

In the spring of 1959 Coach Smith gathered the golf team together in the campus gym and told us that when we practiced would be up to us. He wasn't going to be out there with us much. We should arrange matches with one another to determine what our positions on the team would be. All of us, he added, should make a point of introducing ourselves to the club professional so that he would know we were on the team and not charge us greens fees.

So I walked out to the Pine River Country Club to introduce myself to the pro. The sign beside the door to the pro shop read, "Frank Pegler, Golf Professional." *Frank Pegler*, that name seemed vaguely familiar, and so did his friendly face. "I used to know a Pritchard family," he said. "It was ten years or so ago, when I was pro at Rolling Green in Saginaw."

Rolling Green! This was the golf course my parents dragged me to in the summer of my fifth year, when we lived in the Bancroft Hotel in downtown Saginaw. Frank Pegler was the pro who became a good friend with them that summer. That fall we moved to

Bay City, but we were back in Saginaw the next year; and for the next several years Frank Pegler and my parents frequently played golf together. He also gave my brother his first golf lessons, $12 worth at $2 a lesson, paid for with wages Peter earned delivering the *Saginaw News*.

"Your father was quite a golfer," he said, "often under par at Rolling Green." He added that my mother had a good swing and that my older brother seemed to have gotten off to a good start, too. "You were probably too young to be much interested, but no doubt you've caught up with them by now."

Well, I wasn't going to give Frank Pegler a chance to find out. Peter's lessons began with the 8-iron. He called it his "magic club," serving as 8-iron, 9-iron, pitching wedge, and sand wedge. It had been my 8-iron for the past five years, but I still hadn't figured out how to use it properly under any circumstances. I certainly didn't want to reveal that shortcoming to Frank Pegler nor did I want to give him reason to think that I couldn't match Peter's skills with the other irons he'd passed on to me in 1954.

Maybe Peter had taken lessons from a pro, but I hadn't. I'd learned my imperfect swing the hard way, working on tips from Tommy Armour's *How to Play Your Best Golf all the Time.* Although I worked summers there in high school, I always made sure that Old Mac, my boss and club pro at Hickory Hill, didn't get a close look at my swing.

Luckily, none of the tees were in full view from the pro shop at Alma's Pine River Country Club. It wasn't that I feared that Frank Pegler might mess up my well-crafted swing. Quite the opposite. I feared its fatal flaws would finally be exposed. I wasn't willing to risk finding out that I'd spent five years misinstructing myself in a game that obviously had come to mean so much to me.

I had thought that Gordie Snyder skipping his senior season would spare me from having to contend, once again, with the shadow of my big brother Peter. However, Frank Pegler brought it back. Not only that, now I was revisiting my father, Heyward Pritchard, whose all-around natural athletic prowess cast a large shadow over both of his sons.

Post Hoc

Post hoc, ergo propter hoc ("after this, therefore because of this") is a common logical fallacy that for years I have pointed out to my logic students. Just because one event follows another closely in time, it doesn't follow that the first event causes the second. To fall for this fallacy is to lay the groundwork for false belief, even superstition.

I had an early introduction to the mischief of the *post hoc* fallacy. There was more than golf in the summer of my fifth year at the Bancroft Hotel in Saginaw. That's when I learned that I hated chocolate ice cream. A family friend bought me a chocolate ice cream cone every day—until the day I threw up. For the next 13 years I swore off chocolate ice cream.

I used the same logic with creamed corn when I was eleven. My grandmother, who had the misfortune of witnessing the event, later tried to convince me that it wasn't the creamed corn that made me sick. Although she didn't say it in Latin, she informed me that I was committing the *post hoc, ergo propter hoc* fallacy, one event following another doesn't necessarily mean that the first event caused the second.

It took me a few more years to summon the courage to apply her lesson about the *post hoc* fallacy to eating creamed corn and chocolate ice cream once again. Admittedly, one event following another doesn't *necessarily* mean that the first event caused the second, but that doesn't mean it *couldn't* have caused it. I wasn't ready to take a chance.

However, there was a time when I *deliberately* exploited the psychological power of the *post hoc* fallacy. When I first took up golf as a teenager, I joined my peers in developing the fine art of swearing at golf balls, golf clubs, sticks, stones, sand traps, woods, wind, water, rain, sun—anything but myself. This was a way of testifying to the world that I was an excellent golfer, despite the fact that, at present, I was not performing up to par. I cured myself of throwing golf clubs during high school. I realized such tantrums actually resulted in my playing worse. I also learned they could be costly. My second broken club finally sealed this lesson. But as a college freshman I was still afflicted with cursing. I then decided only drastic measures could cure me of this unseemly, disruptive habit.

I decided to make myself believe that swearing would cause me bad luck. I would convince myself that mere utterance of even the mildest obscenity would bring on a golfing disaster. It's not that cursing would cause me to be distracted. No, it would have to be *bad luck*, rather than lack of proper concentration or effort on my part. I decided to try this out in one of our college golf matches. For the first fifteen holes it worked better than I could have hoped. My concentration was keen and my scores were under control. I was doing well.

However, the sixteenth hole proved to be a severe test. Most of my golf clubs had been inherited from my brother. I still hadn't figured out how to hit my 8-iron more than 80 yards with any regularity, so I used my trusty 7-iron to substitute for it. Over my five years of golf I had specialized in adapting to the shorter distances by shortening my backswing and choking up on the grip. If any club in my bag was indispensable, it was my 7-iron. Then disaster struck.

I was faced with a 150-yard shot to the sixteenth green. What club should I use? I couldn't trust my seldom used 6-iron. It didn't match the other clubs. I carried it mainly so that it would look like I had nearly a full set of clubs. My 5-iron was really best at 160 yards or more. Less than that required a rather drastic change in my swing. Better to press the seven than shorten up on the five, I thought. My swing through the ball felt terrific—a final, sweet burst of power at impact—but as I looked up I saw *two* objects flying in the direction of the green.

I watched in disbelief as my ball nose–dived into a fairway sand trap not more than 50 yards in front of me. But what was that other object, the one flying straight over the trap, dead-aim on the flag? As my eyes turned to my club I realized that it had been beheaded! The head of my beloved 7-iron had sailed 20 yards beyond the ball.

Remarkably, I retained my composure. Perhaps I was in shock, but my swearless streak remained intact. Two 8-irons and two putts later I was in the hole with a double-bogie 6. As I was nearing the seventeenth green I paused to talk with one of my teammates on an adjacent hole. He asked me how I was doing. I replied, "I was doing pretty well until sixteen. But you won't believe what happened. On my second shot, the head of my 7-iron went further than the ball. The *damned* head broke right off!"

I was doomed. The streak broken, my curse would soon be upon me. I bogied seventeen, not great, but I was satisfied. My drive on eighteen went long and down the right side of the fairway. So far, so good. As I approached my second shot, I nervously ran my hands over my irons. One hundred forty yards ahead was the green. Another ten yards beyond the green was the parking lot, out-of-bounds. Beside the green was a gathering of players who had already finished and Coach Smith, eager to see how his freshman would handle the pressure of an audience on his final approach.

I reached for my 7-iron, forgetting for a moment that it was only a headless shaft. Then I realized my fate was sealed. What could I do now? Too far for a 9-iron; it had to be my seldom-used 6-iron, truly a misfit under these circumstances! Short backswing, but how short? Choke up, but how much? Just *do* it. I swung and watched the ball roar in the direction of the green, then over the green on the fly and into the parking lot. My heart sank—out-of-bounds on the last hole, right there in front of the coach and an audience of howling onlookers. "*Damn*, the curse struck!"

But then I heard a loud smack and saw my ball, magically, bounce off a car and roll back onto the green. *Post hoc*. The second curse must have undone it! I calmly sank my second putt for a closing par. All I had to do now was remember to swear in pairs.

Sandbagging

Although I learned the meaning of the word "sandbagging" at the Bloomfield Hills Country Club in the summer of 1958, I doubt that anyone really thought I was sandbagging all summer long. That's a long time to mess up on purpose. Besides, deliberately hitting "shanks" like mine would be difficult. It's a lot easier to strike the ball somewhere on the face of the club than to hit it on the thinnest part of the club *and* have the shot look just like a real shank.

But the next summer I did try sandbagging—at work, not golf. My roommate Terry and I were hired for the summer to work on the Alma College maintenance crew. Apparent subscribers to the Protestant Ethic (after all, Alma was a Presbyterian college), we took a no-nonsense approach to each assigned task. Our boss, Pete Weatherbee, joked that if we didn't slow down, we'd work ourselves out of a job. At least we thought he was joking. Later we found out he was trying to make a serious point.

Meanwhile, our job assignments began to border on the bizarre. We were told that the wooden guard posts around the parking lots weren't lined up properly and needed to be painted. So, our job was to straighten them up and saw off the tops of any that stood taller than the others, and then paint them all.

We finished that job in two weeks, but Pete seemed disappointed. "OK," he said, "See if you can do this one right. The steam pipes run a few feet underground. We need to locate where two of them are connected." We were instructed to dig a deep trench around one steam pipe and proceed until we met the other. Pete then pointed us in the direction we should start. After a full week of digging, we still hadn't found the connection. Pete then suggested we go in the opposite direction. After an hour of digging, we found the other steam pipe.

"Do you think Pete knew which way the pipe was, all along?" asked Terry. "Was he playing some kind of joke on us?"

"Nah," I replied. "Why would he waste our good work on a stupid joke like that?"

Our next job was to carry all the wooden tablet armchairs from the classrooms on the first three floors of Old Main up to the attic. This was so that the floors could be waxed. After a couple of weeks, we were sent back to the attic with the instruction to clean the chairs before bringing them down. That's when we discovered that the attic was a pigeon roost—and that the chairs were covered with hardened pigeon poop.

"Haven't you guys figured out what's going on yet?" one of the long-time maintenance men asked us. "You need to learn how to make a job last. Pete's the boss, and he can't tell you that in so many words. You're driving him nuts working so hard. He's having a hard time thinking up things for you to do. Slow down so that you don't work us all out of jobs."

So, that was it. Don't work so hard; make the jobs last. Well, that would be easy enough. So Terry and I took paperback novels with us to work. We'd work as usual for a while. Then we'd sit in the shade of a tree and read for a while. This was more like it, we thought: work, read, work, read, work, read....

We soon heard, however, that Pete wasn't pleased with this routine. "You have to *look* busy all the time," said one of the long-term maintenance men. You're going to get Pete in trouble. His boss made him hire you guys because you need the money to stay in college a couple of years. Then you'll go off and get cushy jobs somewhere. But this is it for us—this is how we make our living. If you make it look like there isn't enough work to do around here, we're all going to lose out."

"Why'd the college hire so many of you if there really isn't enough work for you?" we asked.

"Well, sometimes we do need all of us around," he replied. "You never know when there will be a job that needs all of us, so we're always ready. But we also know how to make a job last when we need to."

"But why can't everyone just be honest about it?" we objected, "Sure, the college needs to have a full staff available at all times; you never know when they'll all be needed. That makes sense, but why not just be open about it?"

"Because it just doesn't look good to have a bunch of people getting paid while they're standing around doing nothing. We've got to *look* like were needed around here all the time."

That's when I told Terry about the new word I'd learned last summer at the Bloomfield Hills Country Club. "It's *sandbagging*, Terry. That's what we're supposed to be, sandbaggers!"

And that's what we were for the next two summers—two long, long summers of making our jobs last.

Visiting Kalamazoo

Most of Alma College's away golf matches were day trips. The Michigan Intercollegiate Athletic Association schools were within easy driving distance of one another, as were non-conference foes Ferris State and Central Michigan universities. However, we finished each season with an overnight trip to Kalamazoo for the final All-Conference meet, Field Day. At daybreak the next morning the seven MIAA schools would square off at the Kalamazoo Country Club for thirty-six holes.

We always stayed in the Columbia Hotel, just a few blocks from the nation's first pedestrian mall, which had recently opened. Arriving in late afternoon, we'd play a practice round at Milham Park Golf Course, then one of the finest municipal courses in the state. More than four decades later, the faded lettering, "Columbia Hotel," can still be seen on the side of building that hosted us each spring. The pedestrian mall recently was recently reopened to one-way traffic in hopes that this would help restore business to the city center, victim of the proliferation of suburban malls.

However, Milham Park Golf Course remains one of the finest municipal courses in the state.

On my first visit to Kalamazoo, I was introduced to bowling. After a 160 first game, I thought there wasn't much to it. After a second game of 95, a sore right shoulder, and an aching thumb, I realized I had underestimated bowling and I hoped I hadn't jeopardized my golf game for the next day.

Apparently one year I was so focused on the impending match that one of my teammates joked that I probably sleep with my golf clubs. That thought had never occurred to me before. So I tried it out, for the first and last time.

Coach Smith always made sure we arrived at the Kalamazoo Country Club just before sunrise. Undaunted by fog and heavy dew, 35 golfers readied themselves to tee off at the first sign of daylight. This was far and away the best-conditioned golf course we had played all year, and it was all ours for an entire day.

Little did I know that just a few years later I would move to Kalamazoo to teach Philosophy at Western Michigan University, a job which I hold to this day. We even live within a mile of the Kalamazoo Country Club. I drive by this beautifully maintained private course nearly every day, sometimes on the way to Milham. I had an opportunity to play at the country club in the summer of 2002, some 40 years after playing my final college match there. In anticipation, I mentally rehearsed each of its eighteen holes, only one of which had undergone substantial changes. I even recalled a few Field Day shots. This did nothing to enhance my performance, but it was a nice trip down memory lane.

Still, when all is said and done, it's hard to beat Milham and Eastern Hills, Kalamazoo's newer municipal course. Public golf at a public price—that's my kind of golf.

Custom-Fitted Clubs

In 1959 my irons were a hodge-podge. The original matched set of Gormans that Peter passed on to me was falling apart. Only four were left, the 2-, 4-, 5-, and 8-irons—and I didn't know how to use the eight. The 3-iron's head snapped off when I took a wild swing and punched a hole in the bottom of my golf bag two years earlier. My 7-iron lost its head in a golf match that spring. My 9-iron was only a few years old, but it didn't match any of the others. My Silver Scot Tommy Armour 6-iron was a favorite because it bore the signature of the author of the only instructional golf book I'd ever read, but it was a total mismatch with the others. No wonder I'd struggled to become fifth man on Alma College's golf team.

However, there was nothing I could do about it. My scholarship and part-time campus job had been barely enough to get me through the first year of college. Everything I earned from my summer maintenance job at the college had to go toward next year's expenses, which included a raise in tuition. As it turned out, I paid for all my college expenses during the four years I spent at Alma—with two exceptions. First,

I still owed $42 at graduation time, forcing me to take a loan from the college. Second, my mother and brother bought me a new set of irons.

My Christmas present in 1959 was a set of custom-fitted Gorman irons—Top-Kick, knurl lock, pro line irons. Peter had bought his Gormans in Saginaw, when he was in junior high. He'd saved up money from his paper route. But now that he was out of college and working in Detroit, he'd found out that Gormans are made in a little factory on the corner of Telegraph and 12 Mile roads. Even better, at the factory they custom-fit clubs for those who stopped by to be measured. All I had to do was visit the factory, take a few swings to determine the appropriate length and stiffness of the clubs' shafts. At nearly 6' 2", I had an extra inch added to the shafts. Since I found it difficult not to swing harder than I should, I ordered stiff shafts. I used those irons for the next 28 years, and right now I store them in our garage.

I have no doubt that my new Gormans were largely responsible for my becoming first man on the golf team in 1960. My recollection is that those eight irons cost about $100, not much at all by today's standards, but quite a bit for my mother and brother, neither of whom had high paying jobs at the time. I also remember seeing a copy of part of the IRS tax form that my brother helped my mother prepare for 1960. It claimed a deduction for the cost of the golf clubs. To justify this deduction, my brother wrote that playing on the college golf team was an important part of my education, that I desperately needed satisfactory equipment, and that, after all, I was first man on the team!

I have no idea if this plea was successful; and, more than 40 years after the fact, Peter doesn't even remember making it. But if it was successful, I guess beating Baldie at Field Day that year with a 34 on the last nine was important. I doubt that the case would have been nearly as effective if I had been No. 2, not to speak of No. 5.

If it wasn't successful, this may have had something to do with my mother's growing disenchantment with the IRS. Soon she simply stopped filing. We never understood how she managed to avoid the IRS all those years and then resurface to collect Social Security payments for the last 15 years of her life!

Baldie

Richard "Baldie" Baldwin joined Alma College's golf team during my sophomore year. His swing was smooth and unhurried. Despite the effortlessness of his swing, his drives were long and straight. He frequently commented that I'd be better off slowing down my swing. "Where I come from," he'd say, "a swing like that is a sure ticket for the pines." True, we were playing at Alma's Pine River Country Club, but he assured me that this was no match for Grand Haven's narrow, pine-lined fairways.

I must admit that I envied Baldie's accuracy off the tee. Still, I had fought my high school coach's similar advice for too many years to change now. It's not that my driving never got me into trouble. But by then my recovery tactics were well-honed enough that my scores came out pretty much the same as when I hit the ball down the middle. I could scramble out of the rough or woods for pars, bogies, and double bogies. I could also hit 250-yard drives down the middle and fluff an easy second shot or even a third. Also, I wasn't beyond taking an extra putt or two, no matter where my drive landed. Besides, occasionally I'd forget who I was and pick up a birdie or two. So I figured it all averaged out. That was just about it—an average game.

Playing a round with Baldie was always a challenge. In practice rounds he would start out by reminding me of the advantages of swinging easily. He would "ooh" at the length of my sometimes errant drives on the first few, more wide-open holes, making sure that his fell just short of mine—but right down the middle.

At about the fourth hole, a short par three, with an out-of-bounds on the left and a trap in front of the green, he would bring up the subject of *THINKING*. Knowing that I majored in philosophy, he'd comment on my undoubted wisdom, at the same time confessing that he just couldn't get into all that deep thinking. Too much work. That's why he liked golf, he'd say. No thinking—just walk up and hit the ball. Then he'd ask me how I could do it, "Turn off the thinking, just like that?" He'd add something like, "Why, I'll bet you're thinking *all* the time, aren't you? No telling how good you'd be at this game if you'd just stop *thinking* about how to swing at the ball, how to stay out of woods, how to avoid hitting a duck hook, a fat iron—or a shank. Once I worried about hitting a shank—and, sure enough, it happened. But I learned. I'm sure glad I'm no philosopher!"

By the fifth hole Baldie was ready for the kill. There before us was a par 5, occasionally reachable in two shots with the help of a gale-force wind—provided one could hit a long, straight drive that landed in the narrow-necked fairway between dense trees on both sides, with out-of-bounds on the left. Then Baldie would say, "I *love* this hole. Just like my old home course. A real *challenge*—got to keep it straight!"

If he drove first, it was worse. He would add to the pressure by hitting long, right down the middle. But it didn't really matter. I was ready to fold anyway. The match was over.

As luck would have it, we were never paired together that year in our matches against other colleges. Although he regularly beat me in practice matches, he never could best me in matches against other teams. The league meet was his last chance. All seven MIAA colleges met each year at the Kalamazoo Country Club for a final, 36-hole match. Baldie was certain he would beat me this time.

We compared notes as the day progressed. After eighteen, he had an 80 to my 83. We both had 40 on the first nine of our second round. My group finished before his, so I walked out to meet him as he was finishing. Before I could say a word he announced, "I've finally got you! I par in for another 40. I *know* you didn't beat 160. You'd have to have a 36, and you've never done that." "You're right," I said, "I didn't shoot 36."

I stood back as he put his second shot on the par 5 within easy range of the green. Then he turned to me and asked, "So, how'd you do?" "One fifty-seven," I replied, watching his mouth drop in disbelief. "I had 34 on the last nine, three-putting the tenth and eighteenth! I was unconscious, best round I've *ever* had."

I didn't tell Baldie about my rushed swings. My drive on the short tenth hole carried to the back of the green. I three putted for a par. Frustrated at missing an easy birdie putt, I took my fury out on the next tee by hitting a low duck hook that left me with a treacherous sidehill, uphill lie, 120 yards from the hole on the short, 300-yard eleventh. As I was about to hit my second shot, it began to rain. We decided to head for shelter. But first, I said, I would take my shot. Hardly pausing to let my wedge rest behind the ball, I swung wildly. Another low screamer (a "skulled" wedge), my ball slammed into the bank in front of the green, flipped onto the green, struck the flag a few inches above the hole, and dropped straight down for an eagle two!

Standing on the seventeenth tee, I thought about the fact that I was one under par on the back nine with only two holes to go. I had never broken par for nine holes in a competitive round. Temptation lay ahead—a dogleg left, just right for a long hook. Another birdie danced in my head. But *think*, I said to myself. Out-of-bounds and trees on the left—*don't* pull the ball. For me, this was always a formula for a quick swing—get it over with *now*. Whoosh—the ball duck-hooked into the trees, ending up two feet from the out-of-bounds line, with nothing but trees, traps, and a hill between my ball and the green.

Time to gamble. Although I couldn't actually see the green, I saw a sliver of light in its direction. I went for it with a low, 5-iron chip. It wasn't until I was nearly to the green that I saw my ball sitting two feet from the hole. Another birdie! The rest was anti-climactic, as I nervously three putted for a bogie on the eighteenth in front of a small audience of players and coaches.

Baldie's opponents weren't so fortunate. He never missed an opportunity. On the last hole of one match his opponent "gave" himself a six-inch putt, a common practice in casual rounds, but technically unacceptable in matches. Putting his ball in his pocket, the opponent said, "I got a 5."

"No you didn't," retorted Baldie, "you're still putting." At Baldie's insistence, the opponent had to put his ball back down, putt it in, and accept a two-stroke penalty—thus enabling Baldie to win the match!

On another occasion his opponent repeatedly asked Baldie after he hit, "What club did you use?"—another violation of match rules. Reminding him of the rule apparently had no effect on the opponent. Finally, Baldie took matters into his own hands. He hit first on a 180-yard par 3, placing his shot nicely on the green. When asked what club he had used, Baldie simply showed his opponent his club—a wedge! Unnerved by a 180-yard wedge shot, his opponent soon unraveled. Another win for Baldie. His trick was to close the face of his wedge to get a lower trajectory and more distance.

Two years later he played the same opponent on the same course. Apparently his opponent's memory left something to be desired. As Baldie prepared to hit his drive on the same par 3, his opponent told the story of playing against someone a couple of years ago who had driven the green with a wedge! Baldie calmly proceeded to drive the green. Asked what club he had used, he once again held up his wedge. Another win for Baldie.

The Gray Fox

Jim Northrup, professional baseball's Gray Fox (because of his prematurely gray head of hair), played 12 years in the major leagues. He had a distinguished career, but his most memorable year was 1968 when he led the World Champion Detroit Tigers in total hits and RBIs. In May and June he broke up three no-hitters by opposing pitchers. He established a major league record by hitting three grand-slam home runs in a single week, including two in the same game (matching another major league record). He hit another grand slam in the sixth game of the World Series against the St. Louis Cardinals. Then he had a dramatic two-run triple in the deciding seventh game.

Prior to playing for the Tigers, Jim Northrup played on Alma College's golf team. Hailing from St. Louis, he was a multi-sport star at this little 700-student college. This was St. Louis, Michigan, not the home of the Cardinals. This St. Louis was smaller than Alma, a city of 9,000 just three miles down the road, but larger than Breckenridge, Michigan, his birthplace. Why he came to little Alma College rather than traveling 18 miles to Central Michigan or 50 miles to Michigan

State University isn't clear to me. Alma College offered no athletic scholarships, only opportunities for those not good enough for "big time" college sports.

Jim Northrup was certainly good enough to play "big time" college sports. An All-Conference wide receiver in football, he switched to quarterback when the previous year's quarterback didn't return, leading the nation's small colleges in total offensive yardage. Nevertheless, he turned down offers to quarterback for the Chicago Bears and New York Titans, and signed on with the Tigers instead.

We were teammates on Alma College's basketball team during the fall of my freshman year for three days. Having spent too many years riding the pine for my high school, I had no intention of going out for basketball at Alma. However, I still loved the game. One day Wayne Hintz, the basketball coach, saw me sinking baskets in the gym. He introduced himself to me and encouraged me to come out for the team. In addition to having a decent range of shots, somehow I had increased my jumping ability by six inches since high school. So, I decided to give it a try.

It didn't take long for me to realize that, as a freshman, I'd be spending another long season on the pine. I also knew that, although I had an academic scholarship, I needed to work as well. I worried that I wouldn't have enough time left to study so I thanked the coach for his invitation, but told him that I'd have to settle for intramural basketball.

Despite the small size of the Alma campus, I didn't really get to know Jim Northrup well until the spring he showed up at Pine River Country Club, announcing that he was taking up the game of golf and hoped to make the team. How odd, we thought. What was a prospective major league baseball player doing coming out for the golf team during baseball season? Well, he and the baseball coach had a disagreement, resulting in Jim leaving the team. What could he do now? Why not learn how to play golf?

Why not, indeed? We needed five players on the team. Rich ("Baldie") Baldwin, Jim ("Greenie") Greenless, and I could be counted to shoot in the high 70s or low 80s. Bruce Gardner could be counted on to score in the low to mid-90s, but there was no one else around who could break 100. Jim announced that he was determined to break 100 by the end of the season. Since his first efforts were well over 100, this seemed a very ambitious goal, even for such a stellar athlete, especially in Michigan spring weather.

To compound matters, Jim insisted that he play left-handed. We told him it would be a lot easier for us to help him if he, like us, would swing from the right side. "You throw right-handed and shoot baskets right-handed," we pointed out.

"Yes, but I bat left-handed."

"Greenie throws left-handed and shoots baskets left-handed, but he golfs right-handed. So, why don't you give it a try?"

"Because I bat left-handed."

Had we foreseen all those grand slams, the big triple, and the home run he hit out of Tiger Stadium in 1969, we might have better understood Jim's unwillingness to hit from the right side. In any case, we never saw anyone work as hard at trying to break 100 as Jim did that spring. He took our advice (making appropriate translations from right to left). He was good-humored, friendly and, most surprising of all for Alma's "king of sports," as Baldie called him, humble.

On the eve of Field Day, the final 36-hole conference match in Kalamazoo, it was still doubtful that Jim could be counted on to break 100, especially at the Kalamazoo Country Club. However, to everyone's delight, he did it—twice, 97 and 93!

Field Day was scheduled in tandem with the conference tennis championship in Kalamazoo. The tennis competition always took two days. Coach Smith decided he would stay overnight to watch the second day, so he asked if we'd be willing to take his car back to Alma. He'd ride back with the tennis team, he said. Jim immediately volunteered to drive us; he knew all the back roads and would get us there in no time. It was a wild ride, with Jim wheeling around corners and recounting how he'd managed to shoot his two best rounds of the spring.

Baldie was very quiet for the entire trip, much of it spent with his head down. Perhaps he was tired, I thought, or still trying to figure out how I ended up with a lower score again. Forty years later Baldie told me what was really going on. He said it was the most terrifying car ride he'd ever been on, and that he'd spent the entire trip silently repeating the Lord's Prayer to himself more times than he could count!

Terry

Alma College was filled with surprises. For example, although college was supposed to be tougher than high school, less time was actually spent in the classroom, and individual classes met only every other day instead of five days a week. "What were we supposed to do with all that spare time?" I asked. Study—two hours for every hour spent in the classroom—so that's what I did, at least until mid-terms of my first semester.

Mid-terms were a real disappointment. I had over-prepared. How could they ask so little when I had studied so much? So, I decided to cut back a bit, but not in General Chemistry, the one class in which the tests made me realize that I'd never know enough to feel satisfied with the results. I continued to underline every page and then write up careful notes on the leading ideas. Through hard work I managed to carry an A average into the final exam. So did my roommate Terry, but he hardly ever opened the textbook.

"How could he do it?" I wondered.

The answer was simple. Terrence Mark Leichti was brilliant, the smartest person I'd ever met. We all took some college aptitude tests as a part of freshman orientation. Terry's scores were "off the charts," he was told. A few years later he took the Miller Analogies Test and received the highest score one of my psychology professors had ever seen.

The final exam in my first semester of General Chemistry was a different kind of disappointment. I was certain that I failed the multiple-choice, nationally-normed test. I was not surprised to learn that I had gotten only 60 percent of the answers right. The surprise was finding out that the professor converted my score to the equivalent of 100 percent. I had received one of the top scores in the class. In fact, only two students had scored higher. One student's raw score was an astounding 94 percent. Terry, who still had hardly opened his book, scored 86 percent. "Yes," Terry conceded, "there were some tough questions. But they didn't seem to give the guy with the 94 much difficulty."

We soon found out why the other student had done so well. Somehow he had gotten his hands on an answer sheet before taking the exam. Worried that he was going to fail the class, he memorized most of the answers. When he discovered how low the other students' scores were, he realized that the professor suspected foul play. So, he confessed. He also apologized to Terry for making his 86 seem less impressive than it actually was. "I shouldn't have memorized quite so many answers," he said.

Terry had a knack for making the complex seem simple, particularly in math. He saw how to solve problems in the shortest, most elegant manner I could imagine. This turned out to be a shortcoming in his heated arguments with our classmate Dave. Dave and Terry hardly saw eye-to-eye on any controversial topics. I frequently found myself mediating their disputes, trying to get both to see that neither of them was as hopelessly off the mark as they thought. Later Terry would say to me, "Pritchard, I can't believe you thought there was *anything* to Dave's argument; what a dope he can be sometimes. As for you, can't you make up your mind about anything? All this 'on the one hand on the other hand' stuff drives me nuts."

Terry began as a Physics major, but he became bored with lab work. So, he switched to Mathematics until solving math problems bored him. His grades suffered to the point that his Ford Scholarship could easily have been taken away. However, it never was. All it took for Terry to have it renewed was to chat for a while with Dr. William Boyd, Dean of the Faculty. I never knew quite what they talked about—other than Terry's growing list of C's, D's, and E's—but evidently Dean Boyd was impressed by what he heard from Terry.

Finally, Terry turned to Philosophy. Shortly after he'd enrolled in his first Philosophy class as a junior, he confessed, "Pritchard, I really didn't see why you kept trying to give Dave credit in all those arguments, but now I'm beginning to see that some things are a lot less cut-and-dried than I thought." He received a C in Introduction to Logic, but only because he never turned in any homework. After five years at Alma, he graduated with an overall grade point average of C.

Despite his unimpressive grades, Terry probably learned more at Alma College than any student who has ever attended there. Until his senior year in high school, he lived in an orphanage and hardly ever went outside its walls. His parents were killed in an automobile accident when he was three years old. For his last year in high school, he lived with an aunt and uncle in Mt. Clemens, Michigan. By his own account, he had lived a very sheltered life prior to coming to Alma. When he became bored with his classes at Alma, he simply stopped doing any of the required work. Instead, he poured over books in the library, and gave himself a thorough introduction to classical music.

As Terry developed his intellectual talents, I tried to convince him to broaden his interests to include sports. He had no interest in football, volleyball, basketball, or tennis. He did take up ping-pong, and we played lots of rousing games.

Convincing Terry that there was any merit to golf was a much harder sell, however. I finally persuaded him once to walk around the course with me while I played. We started out on Pine River's fifth tee, the spot closest to the Alma campus. Terry insisted that he would not take a swing; he was there only to watch. Finally heading back in the direction of the campus, we came to the fourth hole, a 135-yard par 3. I placed a ball on a tee, handed him my 3-wood, and asked him to see what he could do. To my surprise, he asked me how to grip the club, took a couple of practice swings, and sliced a low line drive toward the road on our left. Then we watched his ball bend back to the right, land just short of the green, and bound 30 feet past the pin—still on the green. He sank the putt for a birdie!

As we walked back to the campus, Terry showed no particular excitement over his unusual accomplishment. It was the first and only time he played golf at Alma—and probably his last time ever. How could anyone expect him to waste his time at such a simple, boring game?

No doubt I envied Terry's brilliance. Evidence of this was a dream I had about his doctoral dissertation. Terry's graduate record in Philosophy was marked with incompletes, first at the University of Michigan, then at UCLA. While he was at UCLA, I dreamt I was visiting him. His wife, Ethel Fay, told me that Terry was nearly finished with his dissertation. I commented that it would be just like him to do it all on a single page, proving something profound in a small set of simple steps. Ethel Fay then announced that it was baking in the oven and should be ready. Out it came, a single slab of clay. But it wasn't done. I woke up with giggling with the thought that it was a half-baked dissertation!

In reality, Terry somehow finally managed to complete his Ph.D., a condition for his first teaching job, at Rutgers University. I asked Ethel Fay what happened to his incompletes. She said that they were "forgiven," and he was allowed to go on to write his dissertation. By this time the job market for philosophers had tightened considerably. Terry told me that he hadn't actually applied for the job at Rutgers. They contacted him, inviting him to fly from California to New Jersey for an interview. He replied that he didn't like flying and wouldn't come for the interview, so they offered him the job over the telephone.

Why did such a brilliant fellow come to Alma College as a seventeen-year old freshman? Terry told me that his Ford Scholarship could be used at any Michigan college or university of his choice.

"Why didn't you go to the University of Michigan?" I asked.

"Money," he replied. "I was told I'd get $1200 if I went to Alma, but only $900 if I went to Michigan."

"But, Terry, that's because Michigan's tuition is only 40 percent of Alma's. Either way you'd have $700 left for your living expenses."

For once Terry had no answer. Nevertheless, he did have an answer for one of my "investments." During our first semester at Alma, he asked me if I believed in God. "I do—just in case," I said. "If there is a God, I don't want to lose out by not believing. If there isn't a God, what have I lost by believing?" What could be simpler, more convincing, than this version of

Pascal's Wager, which I somehow picked up without ever hearing of Pascal?

"Pritchard," Terry immediately replied, "that's the stupidest argument I've ever heard. If there is a God, he'd see through it in a flash. Why would God reward someone for believing in him for a reason like that. If there's a God worth believing in, he'd sooner reward an honest disbeliever." Ah, the *integrity* of belief. That should count for something, shouldn't it?

Traps

Expectations were particularly high for Alma College's golf team in the spring of 1962, my senior year. For the first time ever, we had five players capable of breaking 80, making us the favorite to win the league championship. Coach Smith was so excited about our prospects that he accepted an offer from Ted Welgoss to have us stay at his old army base in Kirksville, Missouri, during spring break. Ted had just returned to Alma to finish his senior year, after having left more than 20 years earlier to pursue a career in the army.

Hardly in the Deep South, northeastern Missouri still qualified as south of Alma, so we proudly went off on our "southern" golf trip. This was the first spring golf trip in the history of the Alma College team—it was also the last time an Alma College golf team stayed north of Mason–Dixon line for its spring tune-up.

During our three-day visit to Kirksville, we played golf in rain and snow, with the temperatures never reaching above 45 degrees. Given the inclement weather, the cold army barracks, and the necessity of bundling up in sweaters and jackets, we played surprisingly well. The return trip to Alma took us miles out of our way in order to get across the badly flooded Mississippi River. Had we stayed in Alma, we would have been treated to sunny skies and temperatures in the 60s.

Unfortunately, after returning to the warmth of Alma, I found myself overswinging. Efforts to hit 250-yard drives resulted in 125-yard grounders. Apparently shedding my sweater and jacket gave me too much freedom to swing away. For the next several weeks, I struggled to get my swing under control—and to retain a spot in the top five on the team.

The highlight of the league competition was the annual trip to Kalamazoo for Field Day. All of the Michigan Intercollegiate Athletic Conference teams would face off at the Kalamazoo Country Club for an all-day 36-hole marathon. Half of the points for the league championship were determined by dual matches among the teams. The other half came on Field Day.

We won all of our dual matches. Even a second place finish on Field Day would give us the championship. My game had finally improved enough to earn the fifth spot on the team, and I looked forward to one last trip to Kalamazoo. I had done especially well the previous two years on Field Day. Each time I shot 83 for the first eighteen. As a sophomore I shot my all-time competitive low for the second eighteen, a 74. As I junior I finished the second eighteen with a 78.

But here I was, a senior, barely qualifying for the fifth and final position on the team so that I could take part in Field Day one last time. Once again I had 83 for the first eighteen. I looked forward to repeating the pattern of the previous two years, another round in the 70s. It was not to be. Suddenly I was beset with bogies. I finished the first nine with a disappointing 46. My bogie affliction continued through the first three holes of the final nine.

The next hole was a par 5 dogleg to the right. It was tempting to try to take a shortcut and try for a birdie, but balls that failed to make it were out-of-bounds. I knew better than to risk an out-of-bounds. The previous year I watched a fine golfer from Kalamazoo College take an 18 on that hole. He tried to cut across the dogleg on his first drive—and on his next seven, as well. To his credit, he was one under par for the other eight holes on that nine.

No shortcut for me. Instead, I hit a long drive safely to the left of the shortcut. "At last," I thought, "my game is beginning to come around. A big 3-wood could put me in position for a birdie." Instead, I popped it up into a sand trap some 80 yards from the green. My third shot went into a trap next to the green. My fourth stayed in that trap. Finally, I escaped to the green and three-putted for a triple bogey 8.

Then came yet another bogie. Four holes to go and already 7 over par for the nine. Something had to give—and it did. After a nice drive I was pleased to see my second shot heading for the right side of the green, pin high. Unfortunately, it bounced to the right into the deepest sand trap I'd ever seen. I took my third, fourth, and fifth shots from that trap. I took my sixth, seventh, and eighth shots from the trap on the other side of green. My ninth and tenth shots were taken from the first trap. In all, I took 12 shots on the hole!

I recorded two more bogies, and then realized that I needed to par the last hole in order to break 100. My 70-foot downhill putt dropped in the hole for my first and only par of the nine.

I was 20 shots away from my goal of breaking 80 for my last eighteen, and the team was two shots shy of winning the conference championship. "How could this have happened to me?" I wondered. Terrible as my score was, I felt that this was more a matter of bad fortune than total ineptness. In fact, I was convinced that I could go out the next day and shoot par for nine holes at our home course, even though I had never succeeded in doing so before.

So, the very next day I set out by myself for one last round at the Pine River Country Club. Avoiding trees, rough, water and, most of all, sand traps, I breezed around the course with nine pars. Of course, this wasn't golf under fire, but it did erase some of the sting of the nightmare I'd experienced the previous day.

George

Traverse City Junior High was the third school I'd attended in the seventh grade. The year began in Bay City. But we moved to the Old Mission peninsula in early fall. There I attended a two-room school house. The highlight of that winter was receiving a letter from my Saginaw friend, Dick Thomas. Addressed just to, "Mike, Old Michigan, Michigan," somehow it was hand-delivered to me at the Old Mission post office!

Old Mission was beautiful, but remote and cold. So, the next spring we moved into Traverse City. George Drew and I hit it off right away. He, too, had just moved into Traverse City—from Long Lake. His father had just died, and we both needed a good friend for moral support in a classroom of strangers.

After we finished eighth grade, George and I took up golf together, along with Bucky and Lance. However, after a summer of fun on the links, I moved again, this time to Milford. In the summer after my sophomore year in high school, my mother and I paid a visit to Traverse City to attend the wedding of my brother's old girlfriend (one of the few who met my mother's approval). Only fifteen, I didn't drive yet. However, a lot of my old Traverse City pals did, including George.

In fact, George took several of us for a terrifying ride on Old Mission peninsula. It was almost as frightening as the time my brother, Peter, took me for an 85-mile-an-hour thrill ride down the highway near our home in Bay City. He finally slowed down when the floor board caught on fire.

During my visit, George and I played a round of golf at the Traverse City Country Club. Eager to demonstrate how much our games had improved since starting out together two summers before, neither of us played very well. Halfway through the round, we were joined by Lance. He had new set of Walter Hagen clubs. It was his good fortune that the old golfing legend Walter Hagen had recently retired in the Traverse City area, and his dad was an old friend. So, Lance was getting golfing tips from one of the world's greatest golfers. Lance, too, had his problems on the course that day, but I could see that both Lance and George had vastly improved their games. They had learned how to hit hooks, and I was still slicing my drives; I was envious. And I was sad, for I had to return to Milford.

I didn't know when, if ever, I might visit Traverse City again, nor did I really expect to see George again. So, in my first year at Alma College, I was surprised to learn from Millie that her friend Jane, a freshman at Olivet College, was dating someone named George Drew. George and I were dating high school friends from little Decatur, Michigan! Soon George and I would meet on the golf course, on opposing teams. We never were in the same foursome during our four years of college competition, but we always compared scores—until our last Field Day at Kalamazoo College.

For some reason George had a hard time at Field Day, finding it difficult to break 100 for any of the rounds at our first three Field Day competitions. Basically inconsolable, he said he couldn't understand why everything had suddenly fallen apart. Having done well myself, I didn't know what I might say to offer him some consolation.

However, in our senior year, the tables were turned. George had two good rounds on Field Day. My first round was all right, but the second was a disaster. I had to sink a very long putt on the last hole to break 100. As soon as I finished I thought of George—so *this* is what it feels like to have everything fall apart on the big day.

I looked around for George so that I could congratulate him on finally playing well on Field Day, and to tell him that now I understood what he had gone through those first three years. But he was nowhere to be found. I could only hope that he was finally pleased to finish on a high note. As for me, I now had my own mystery of failure to solve.

I never saw George after that. He once told me that he was majoring in German and Political Science. He hoped to become some sort of foreign diplomat. We both knew that we needed day jobs—and that we should never give them up for golf. Maybe Lance, with his Walter Hagen-aided swing, could take golf more seriously, but he probably knew better, too.

Catching Up With Baldie

More than a quarter century after leaving Alma, I had an opportunity to play Baldie's "home" course, the Grand Haven Country Club. I had not forgotten his admonitions about slowing down my swing for accuracy, but I had still not taken them to heart. I felt some vindication as I watched my first drive soar down the right side of the fairway. No problem! Then my golf partner, an old-hand at playing the Grand Haven course, commented, "Looks like trouble to me." I looked at him in disbelief, then looked back at my ball as it landed in the fairway, and then took a sharp bound to the right—into the pines.

Too bad Baldie wasn't there to see it, I thought. I've finally learned his lesson. I'm going to work on slowing down my swing. I've taken some Hatha Yoga classes. *Very* relaxing. It's mainly lots of stretching and deep breathing, and makes you limber and feel ten years younger. It doesn't involve any of that really *deep* meditation stuff, just enough to clear the head of a lot of clutter.

Now I can think of just one or two things at a time instead of having all kinds of wild thoughts rushing through my head when I'm swinging at the ball. I can get rid of a lot of that *thinking* Baldie knew was messing around with my game. I can't get rid of *all* of it—but when I'm in the right mode, *shank* is the first thought to vanish.

Maybe I'll share these thoughts with Baldie. It might whet his appetite for a challenge. It's really been quite a long time now. Of course, we've both changed a lot, too. After his freshman year at Alma, he quit college for a while. He didn't think the life of the intellect was for him. So, he took up sweeping floors in a factory back home. But then, with all those lonely hours on the late shift in the factory, he found himself *thinking*. And he kind of *liked* it, so much so that he went back to college. Now he has a Ph.D., and is some kind of hot shot in Michigan's Department of Education.

I'll bet he has to think *really hard* at that job. He's probably one of those guys who takes his work home with him at night and on weekends. He probably could use a break. A little round of golf with his old buddy might do him a world of good. Maybe he'll be eager for a rematch—*too* eager. It might even make him swing a little too fast, especially when he sees my new smooth, unhurried, effortless swing. Besides he's a real *thinker* now.

Postscript: I wrote this little story about Baldie in 1988. Ten years later I sent him a copy and we did have a reunion on the golf course—twice. It's true that he's a real thinker now. He's retired from his state-level Department of Education job and is writing mystery novels! Our first "match" was played on one of my "home" courses near Kalamazoo, then it was my turn to visit his.

Apparently he hasn't lost any of his competitive savvy. On the first tee he advised me that, although we couldn't see what lay over the hill ahead, there was nothing to worry about as long as I hit it in the fairway. I'd have to really crunch one to get in trouble. I hit a nice drive down the right side of the fairway. "Oh, oh," I heard Baldie exclaim. We found my ball over the hill, but well to the right of the fairway, behind a set of large trees at the bottom of the precipitous drop where the fairway swerves sharply to the left. "Wow, you really hit that one, Mike," Baldie conceded.

2001

Baldie and I were at it again. Years and years had passed since we played together on the Alma College golf team that went to Field Day with the conference championship "in the bag." Although we had enjoyed a few reunions on the golf course during the intervening years, we had never revisited Field Day 1962.

This was the day that all the MIAA teams gathered for a glorious final thirty-six holes at the Kalamazoo Country Club. Half the season was on the line. Dual matches with each team were completed. We won all of ours that year. All we had to do was finish second on Field Day to win the championship outright. Finally, 39 years later, I broke the ice.

"Remember when we blew the championship in '62?"

"Oh, no!" Baldie quickly replied. "I was hoping you'd forgotten all about that. Now you're going to remind me that I cost us the championship in that last match."

"*You* cost us the championship? Are you serious? I blew it in the sand traps on the fifteenth. Back and forth from one to the other—what a nightmare!"

"You've been blaming yourself all these years? I'm the one who gave up looking for my lost ball when the other guys said it didn't matter—we had it won. I just stopped looking and took a two-stroke penalty. That's what cost us the championship."

Yes, I had been blaming myself all those years. This was one part of my personal history, something I had learned to live with, even laugh about. At the time it was serious stuff. There we were, poised to be the first Alma team to win the MIAA golf championship. How could I shoot a 53 on the last nine? Choke? Why did I finish my college career in such an ignoble manner?

Determined to convince myself that it was just a fluke, I visited our home course the next day for one final round, my best ever at the Pine River Country Club. A fitting finish, just a day too late. So, maybe it was only a bad day, albeit one that would be etched forever in my memory and eventually fuel bittersweet jokes about the wisdom of not giving up my "day job" as a philosophy teacher for a career in golf.

So, what was Baldie's story all those years? He didn't take up golf as his "day job" either. Had he thought much about not continuing to look for his lost ball? Could he have written it off as a fluke, just a bad day? I could play one last round at the home course to prove to myself that I'd just had an off day, something that could happen to anyone.

"But, I should have known better," Baldie might have said to himself again and again. "Every shot counts…."

How do our other teammates remember that infamous day? Did they blame me? "How *could* Pritchard shoot a 53 on the last nine? What a choker." Or Baldie? "Why didn't he look a little longer?" Or themselves? "Why did we think we'd won? We never should have told Baldie that we had it clinched." Or possibly they, too, recall some bad shots they had made. Or maybe, like the rest of the world, they give the matter no thought whatsoever.

Still, known for the next ten years or so as the last Alma team *not* to win the championship, all of us left our mark. The last losers, yet good enough to win. That's something worth remembering—and something for which we can all take credit or blame.

That Which One Cannot Well Leave

I finally made up my mind in my senior year at Alma College to pursue a graduate degree in Philosophy at the University of Wisconsin. It was sometime during my sophomore year that I learned that I was supposed to declare a *major*. This was a challenge. First I had to find out what a major was, then I had to run every conceivable possibility through my mind.

"If you can't figure out what *you* want," suggested a friend, "why not pick Psychology? At least then you could help others figure out what *they* want." So I became a Psychology major—for a few months. Almost immediately, I began to have second thoughts.

I read a little (*very* little) Nietzsche. He seemed rather suspicious of psychologists. They were too nosy, trying to peek under people's skin and things like that. I had to admit that I did feel a little uneasy around some of the psychology majors, especially the sneakier ones. Still, it seemed like a noble profession, trying to understand the human psyche in hopes of improving the human condition.

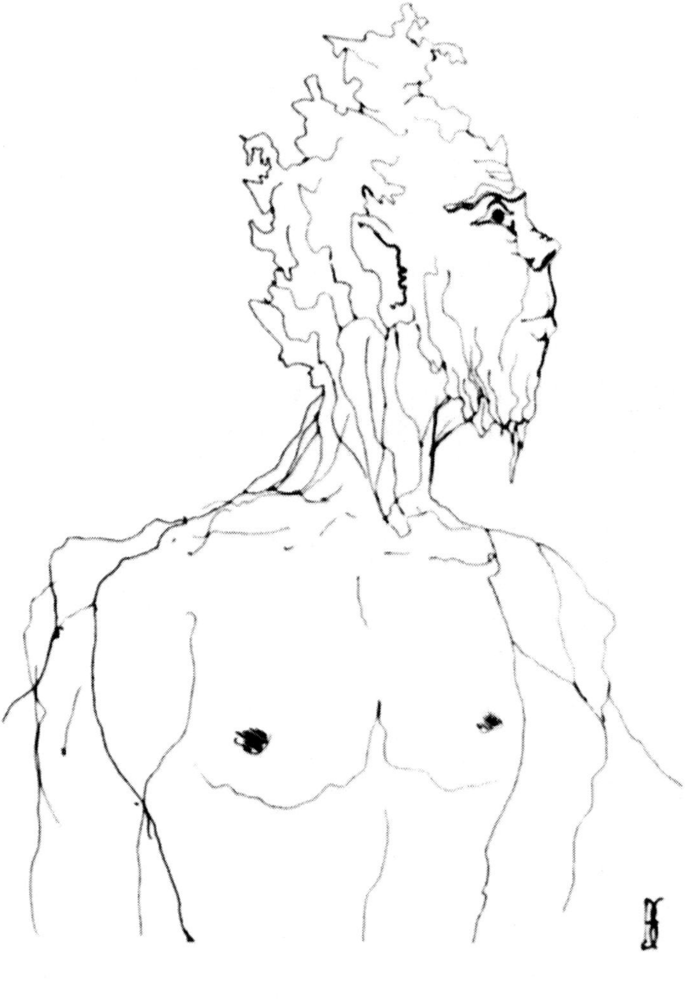

Young Philosopher from Wayne

But the little white rats puzzled me. The first time our Behavioral Analysis class visited the rat lab we were shown a Skinner box. Inside was a rat tapping a bar and running over to a slot in the wall. When the light came on after it tapped the bar, a little dipper of water slid through the slot. No light, no dipper. We noticed that the little white rat didn't run over to the slot nearly so often when the light didn't come on.

"What do you suppose that little white rat is thinking?" asked the lab assistant. That was a tough one, but I gave it a try.

"It's probably thinking that it's a waste of time to go over to the slot when the light doesn't come on," I replied.

"No, *no*, *NO*!" remonstrated the assistant. "You can't say that. Psychology is a *science*. Stick to what you can *observe*. Now, what do you see? You don't see thinking—not the rat's, not mine, not your classmates', not even your own. But it doesn't matter. It's all behavior and reinforcement. 'Thinking' is not a scientific term, and we don't need it to explain anything. This is the first, and most important, lesson in psychology."

Well, that was a surprise, *psych*ology without the psyche. But that might make the whole enterprise more challenging, trying to figure out people's behavior without giving a thought to what they are thinking! Besides, it was a bit of a relief to stick just to people's behavior and not even try to get under their skin.

Studying rats might prove interesting, too. Anatomically, we were told, there are strong analogies between rats and people. Perhaps we would learn the origins of expressions like, "You dirty rat," "He's nothing but a low down rat," and "Don't be a rat-fink." We might even learn some new expressions, such as, "Like a rat, you've been operantly conditioned to behave in ways that almost everyone around you finds aversive."

But my doubts deepened when I went to my first (and only) Psychology convention. The American Psychological Association met in Chicago in the spring of 1960. The Playboy Keyclub had recently opened, and one of my professors had a key. So there I was, barely nineteen, studying bunnies in Chicago and having my first sip of scotch.

Rats and bunnies were not what I had in mind when I chose Psychology as my major. I needed something more *serious*—like Philosophy.

Besides, I learned that a Philosophy major required only 24 credit hours. Psychology, on the other hand, required 32 hours plus a full year of Biology and Math. If I majored in Philosophy, I would have more time for electives. I could still take Psychology classes and, I reasoned, I'd get a broader education this way and have more time for golf.

As a senior Philosophy major and a budding graduate student, I was also a senior playing his last year on the golf team. That posed a serious problem. I knew a lot more about golf than graduate school. My advisor, Wesley Dykstra, suggested that this might be a good time to close the gap a bit. Why not go with him to a philosophers' convention at Wayne State University? I could meet William Hay, Chair of Wisconsin's Department of Philosophy, and get a preview of graduate school.

This seemed like a good idea, except for the fact that I would have to miss a golf match. After much agonizing, I reluctantly agreed to give up the match. I was introduced to William Hay on Friday morning, and we agreed to meet at 2:00 P.M. for a conversation.

He still hadn't arrived at 2:15, nor at 2:30. By 2:45, I made up my mind. I stormed out of the convention and hitchhiked back to Alma for the Saturday golf match. Philosophy could wait.

A few days later I received a note of apology. William Hay said that he was very sorry, but he had gotten involved in "a conversation I could not well leave". Never having been in such a conversation, I had no idea how this was possible—a conversation one could not well leave? About *what*?

Sure, I knew what it was like to get so involved in a discussion of "speculative" philosophy that I didn't even look at the clock on the wall for the entire 50 minutes of Wes Dykstra's class. Still, when the bell rang, the class stopped, except for Jim White and me. We carried on all the way to the next class. Jim had the job of helping Dr. Rex King get to the classroom in his wheelchair to teach us something about the "worldly" philosophy of Adam Smith and other economists, so our discussions always came to a quick and timely ending.

I made the mistake of sharing William Hay's note with Millie, my wife-to-be. She's never forgotten his words. She's been faithfully reciting them ever since, each time I've come home late from "a meeting of the minds."

Why didn't I understand William Hay's comment in 1962? So what if my classmates were always ready to terminate our philosophical conversations at the drop of a pin? So what if I didn't understand how anyone could get *that* wound up in intellectual pursuits?

I knew full well what it was like to get involved in something I could not well leave. During golf season I nearly always made it to the campus dining room just before the doors were locked. Admittedly, I did leave my golf to go to a convention of philosophers. But I didn't *well* leave it—and I got back just in time not really to have left at all.

Wisconsin

Indebtedness

Scheduled to graduate from Alma College in June 1962, I had a serious problem. I had to pay my last bill, $42, to receive my diploma. Virtually penniless, for the first time in my life I faced the necessity of asking for a loan, "Could I borrow $42 from the college if I promise to pay it back in a year—with interest, of course?"

Mr. Kent Hawley, Dean of Students, frowned and leaned forward in his chair. "Aren't you getting married next week?" he asked.

"Yes."

"If you don't have the $42 you owe the college, what do you plan to live on when you are married?"

"Millie and I have graduate fellowships at Wisconsin," I replied. "We start a week after we're married. This will give us each $400 plus our tuition for the summer."

Scratching his head and breaking into a smile, Mr. Hawley offered, "Well, it seems to me you'll need a little money for that first couple of weeks. We won't lend you $42. It has to be $100—a no-interest loan."

I was grateful, but hardly reassured. About to marry, I was already in debt. Unpaid bills, I was told, led to the demise of my parents' marriage. Between us, Millie and I would earn $4800 in tax-free fellowships over the next 12 months. Could I carve $100 out of this to clean my slate? I certainly hoped so.

As the due date approached, Millie and I decided to move from Madison to Stoughton. Millie had finished her master's degree in Spanish and accepted a high school teaching job. I would commute 18 miles from Stoughton to Madison as I continued my doctoral work, but this meant that we needed a newer car. The 1951 Ford Millie's parents had given us would not be up to the commute, especially after it suffered a cracked engine block from Madison's 30 degrees below zero weather during our first Wisconsin winter.

Financial reality set in. One hundred dollars had to be sent to Alma, we needed to buy car, we were moving from a furnished to an unfurnished apartment and needed to buy some furniture, Millie's teaching job and my graduate assistantship wouldn't start until September, and our fellowships had run out. We needed summer jobs. Millie's journalistic background served her well. She was hired as a reporter for the weekly Stoughton newspaper. But what could I do?

Glancing through the job ads in the *Wisconsin State Journal*, one particularly caught my eye:

> Wanted: Summer bartender at
> Stoughton Country Club. No
> experience needed. $300 per mo
> plus free golf. If interested,
> contact Jimmy Midthun, Mid-
> thun Used Car Sales.

My first reaction to this ad was that I could never get such a job. Not only had I never bartended, I was a twenty-two-year old "teetotaller" who didn't know the difference between a martini and a manhattan.

Admittedly, I had taken a little sip of scotch while attending the APA's (American Psychological Association's) annual meeting in Chicago in the summer of 1960. And, to my immediate regret, I had recently gulped down a tiny glass of a distinctly fiery orange liqueur, just a moment before our host advised me to sip it very slowly. How could I present myself as a serious candidate for a bartending job?

Free golf and $300 a month? Surely it was worth a try. Since our move to Stoughton would require us to upgrade our car, I'd explain our dire economic circumstances. To my great surprise, Jimmy Midthun immediately offered me the job. As for my lack of experience with alcohol, he offered two comments. First, he wouldn't have to worry about having a bartender whose drinking interferes with his work. Second, I would be working right beside an experienced bartender who would teach me on the job. Apologizing for the low salary, he added that a real bargain had just shown up in his lot, a year-old Volkswagen Beetle with a sunroof and low mileage. Sold! What Jimmy Midthun didn't realize is that, aided by the lure of free golf, the salary struck me as quite reasonable. The Volkswagen was simply icing on the cake.

Actually, the icing turned out to have more than a little lemon in it. Within a year we had to put in a rebuilt engine. Already making monthly payments of $59.67, we refinanced our loan to $75.99 per month. Tax-free fellowships during our first year of marriage had created a false sense of financial security. We rented a furnished apartment for $100 a month, had a paid-for car that we seldom needed to drive, and paid all our bills on time. Now officially our income was larger, but tax withholdings gave us less take-home money. In Stoughton our rent was higher, and we had to figure out how to finance a bed, a couch, a table and chairs, curtains, kitchen utensils, a car that needed gas, and who knows what else.

My Alma loan may have been behind us, but it was clear that it was only the beginning of much more to come.

Bartending

My first day as a bartender was uneventful—a few beers, some whiskey, and a gin and tonic or two, but no martinis or manhattans. The second day, I was warned, would be more challenging.

Wednesday morning was "Women's Day," I was told. That morning the course would be reserved for women (as compensation for their not being allowed on the course on Saturdays until evening and Sundays until the afternoon). They would play nine holes and then assemble in the bar for lunch and drinks. I was alerted that almost every order would be special in some way—dry martinis, very dry martinis, Tom Collins, whisky sours, an exotic this or that.

During the confusing first hour Carl, the senior bartender, coached my every move. Then came the moment of truth. We were out of ice. "Can you take over for a few minutes, Mike, while I go get some from the ice house next door?"

"Sure, Carl, go ahead." And pleeeease get back here as soon as you can, I silently pleaded.

Somehow I was able to handle the next several requests, but as Carl's absence lingered on, I grew increasingly flustered. "Ginger ale, please," said the young woman. I quickly surveyed the array of bottles behind the bar, but made no visible move. The blank look on my face prompted another, "Ginger ale, please."

"What is it that she wants?" I puzzled to myself.

"It's right there," she said, smiling and pointing to a bottle of ginger ale.

"Oh," I finally realized, "you just want plain ginger ale—without any of that other stuff." I knew all about ginger ale. I even knew about ginger-ale floats. In fact, my first encounter with a ginger-ale float was as a youngster in the clubhouse of another golf course. As I moved closer to inspect my mother's intriguing concoction, I felt a tickling, stinging sensation in my nose as it was invaded by tiny bubbles. Startled, it took me several minutes to summon the courage to revisit this strange brew, but soon I regarded myself as a connoisseur of ginger ales, strongly preferring Detroit's sweet Vernors to Canada Dry and the other pale imitations of the day.

Regardless of their respective merits, I knew the labels well. And there, plainly in view, was a bottle of Canada Dry. Much embarrassed, I had failed to understand the simplest request for which I could have hoped.

The third day on the job was even more challenging. This was the fifth reunion of Stoughton High School's Class of 1958—a clubhouse filled with twenty-three-year olds eager to demonstrate to their old classmates that they could binge drink with the best of them. Several quick drinks into the evening, a tall, heavyset fellow claimed I had shortchanged him. I carefully ran through the calculations for him.

Unconvinced, he repeated his accusation. The exchange heated up, culminating in his suggestion that we step outside to settle the matter, "like men." As I began to mull over his invitation, fortunately he was whisked away by a few of his long-lost buddies. He didn't return to my part of the bar until a couple of hours later, at which point he declared, with drunken sincerity, that I was one of the nicest people he'd ever met—and a great bartender, as well!

Once again we ran out of ice, this time both in the bar and the ice house. "What do we do about ice now, Carl?" I asked.

"When they finish their drinks, we dump the ice in the sink. It's pretty dark in here. Just grab a clean glass, drop it below the bar level, and slip in some of the old cubes. The alcohol will take care of any germs and they'll never know the difference." Reluctant at first, I soon became quite adept at quickly recycling ice cubes into fresh drinks, until I saw a used lime in my customer's bourbon. Before anyone noticed, I retrieved the drink, extracted the lime, slipped in another piece of ice, and presented the drink to the customer as if nothing had happened. After this, I made sure I looked before I slipped.

By the fourth day I began to identify the regulars. Nearly every day the same group of four men came in and rolled dice to see who would pay for the first round of drinks, then the second, the third, and finally the fourth. Charlie was old and frail looking. Otherwise silent, for each round he'd quietly say, "Seltzer and rye." As the other three quickly downed their drinks each round, Charlie continued to nurse his first one and let the others line up. As he sat there, head down and looking as if he was about to doze off, I wondered if he really wanted all those drinks. However, I had been told that he would never leave before consuming all four, which he did. I worried about him in silence as he staggered out of the club each day.

And I worried about Bob, another of the dice rollers, who one day was so inebriated that he couldn't figure out how to open the screen door to leave. He repeatedly pushed against the hinges, muttering that something was wrong with the door.

I worried about these men, but I did nothing to discourage them from drinking to the point of endangering themselves (or others should they get behind the wheel). This, I was told, was not my responsibility. My job was to give the members what they wanted. It was their job to take care of themselves and each other. I was assured that only one member had a real drinking problem, and he seldom showed up at the club. No doubt my inability to remain comfortable with these assessments had much to do with my determination to find other means of support in future summers, free golf or not.

Then there was the woman who told me, again and again, that she was delighted that the club had hired a philosophy student as summer bartender. She'd always ask my advice about this or that psychological problem, and each time I waited patiently for an opportunity to tell her politely that I wasn't studying psychology or psychiatry. My field, I said, is philosophy.

Observing this maneuver several times, John, a high school student working at the club, took me aside and asked, "Well, what *is* philosophy, then?" I offered the standard reply that defining philosophy is itself a philosophical task, and a most difficult one at that. But, I added, we could talk about some philosophical problems.

"Like what?" asked John.

"Like, take a look at that ash tray on the counter there. What color is it?"

"Green."

"Is it *really* green, or does it only *appear* to be green?"

"It looks green to me. Doesn't it look green to you?"

Sensing that my first attempt to introduce John to epistemology and the mysteries of metaphysics was going nowhere fast, I shifted gears a bit. "Of course it *looks* green to me, John. But how do you know that what I *call* green isn't what you would *call* red if you could see through my eyes?"

"Didn't you say it looked *green* to you? Now are you saying it looks *red*?"

"No, I'm just asking how you *know* that you see colors the same way I do."

"Are you trying to play a trick on me? Can you really make it look red?"

"Okay, let's try another example. You hit really long drives, John. Suppose you are playing alone and you hit a ball so far that you can't see it land. You know, 'Out of sight, out of mind.' So, if it's out of your mind, how do you know it exists?"

"Because I find it when I walk in the direction I hit it? But I think I see what you mean. With that big hook of yours, when you hit it out of sight, you may *never* see it again."

"Right, John. So, when I lose a ball like that, how do we *know* it still exists?"

"Hey, is this like that crazy question about whether a tree in the forest makes a sound when it falls and no one is around to hear it? Well, ask the squirrels. I'll bet they'd hear it. As for your golf balls, see those two kids over there? They find them and sell them for 25 cents a piece."

"You're kidding me!"

"No, I'm not. Every evening they look for lost balls in the rough, the woods, and all the places guys like you lose them."

"I can't believe how many balls I've lost this summer."

"Would you like some advice about how to get rid of that hook of yours?"

I should have accepted John's offer. I spent the entire summer trying to figure out how to stop hitting that sweeping hook. So while I learned much about bartending, I can't say the same about golf.

And I obviously had much to learn about how to introduce someone to philosophy.

Pre-Lims

In the spring of 1965 I took my doctoral preliminary examinations in Philosophy at the University of Wisconsin. For each of three days during the week of my pre-lims, I wrote for more than ten hours without benefit of books or notes, trying to answer abstruse questions about History of Philosophy, Metaphysics and Theory of Knowledge, and Ethics. Mentally exhausted, but physically restless, I decided that a ten-hour day of golf would be an appropriate way to cap off the week.

Duane Willard, who had undergone the same ordeal, agreed. Dick Pulaski, who had neither taken the pre-lims nor ever played golf, joined us. I don't recall specifically what convinced Dick on that day. During our three years as graduate students together, we had engaged in several philosophical discussions about the merits of this or that sport. Dick was an excellent all-around athlete, and he was especially good in basketball. I must have said some things about the challenge of golf for even the most gifted athlete that whetted his appetite.

In any case, we all showed up early in the morning at the clubhouse of Middleton Golf Course, high on a windy hill overlooking Madison. The temperature was in the mid-40s, and it dipped into the 30s as snow fell during the day. Dick and I called Duane "Cap'n Crunch," after the muscular figure on the cereal box. Cap'n Crunch said he'd had enough after thirty-six holes. I asked Dick if he'd like to go another nine. Undaunted by either the game or the weather, Dick was quite agreeable.

Some years later Dick and I recalled this unusual day. I said that the pre-lims must have put Cap'n Crunch and me in a crazed state of mind, but why did Dick go along with this? Dick replied that he just thought that's what golf was all about. Playing in those conditions had convinced him that it was a game worthy of being taken seriously!

Later he wondered why golfers were so fussy about the playing conditions. If the Green Bay Packers could play football in sub-zero snowstorms, why couldn't golfers put up with a few snowflakes in the 30s?

Lake Cora

As I made my way around Lake Cora Golf Course, I tried to remember the old layout from more than 20 years before. Somehow it seemed to me that some of the holes had been rearranged, but I couldn't be certain after so many years. A much clearer memory for me was the set of circumstances that brought me to Lake Cora that first time.

It was the summer of 1966, and Millie and I had just helped the Pulaskis move from Sheboygan, Wisconsin, to Kalamazoo. Dick and I had begun graduate study together in Philosophy at the University of Wisconsin in 1962. By 1965 several of us had completed our coursework, and we were offered the opportunity to become half-time instructors at two-year centers of the university. Dick and his family went to Sheboygan; Millie and I went to Manitowoc.

After a year in Sheboygan, Dick decided to take a full-time job at Western Michigan University. He would move his family to Kalamazoo and return to Wisconsin for the summer while finishing his "pre-lims," a set of arduous exams taken before beginning one's doctoral dissertation. The plan was that Dick would spend the summer with us in Manitowoc. He rented a moving van that he and I would return to Sheboygan.

Millie, then very pregnant with Scott, Dick's wife Tweetie, and their five children crossed Lake Michigan on the Manitowoc/Ludington ferry, where they were met and driven to Kalamazoo. Dick and I took the van the long way around the lake.

Dick and I were to drive the van back to Sheboygan, pick up his car, and drive it 32 miles north to Manitowoc. We would meet Millie at the ferry station. Before leaving, we speculated that we could get in a round of golf on the way and still meet Millie in time. Millie declared in no uncertain terms that I would be very, very sorry if she had to wait even one minute for us to pick her up. No problem, we assured her.

Dale Westphal, one of Dick's new colleagues, had helped us unload the van, and he volunteered to guide us to a local golf course "right on the way" to Wisconsin—Lake Cora Golf Course, just a few miles west of Paw Paw and within easy reach of I-94. After finishing nine holes, Dale asked if we wanted to go around one more time. There seemed to be time, but recalling Millie's admonition, I told Dick that it would be far better to be an hour or so early than even the tiniest bit late. I didn't want to take any chances.

So, we continued our journey, confident that we would arrive in plenty of time. Thirty miles later the van rolled to a stop on the side of the road. Seeing that the main gas tank was empty, we tried, unsuccessfully, to shift to the reserve tank. Unable to restart the engine, I waited in the van while Dick hitched a ride to the nearest service station. What a state of affairs. To be on the safe side, we had played only nine holes; but here I was stuck in a broken down van.

A few minutes later I turned on the ignition again. To my surprise, the engine started immediately. Apparently there had been a vapor lock. So I headed down the road to the nearest service station, hoping I would find Dick before he returned with help. Luckily, I found him at the next exit. A small, but worrisome delay, enough to make me wonder if our two-hour side venture at Lake Cora was ill-advised after all. Unanticipated delays driving through Chicago did nothing to alleviate my worries.

By the time we dropped off the van in Sheboygan, it was a toss-up whether we would make it to Manitowoc in time. I told Dick that I knew a shortcut along the lake and that I should drive his car. Years later Dick confided that he found this to be a particularly terrifying ride—nearly 30 miles of winding coastline in the dark at a speed that he had never seen me drive and that he never would have dared himself.

But we did arrive in time. As we approached the harbor from an overlooking hill, we could see the lights of Millie's ferry about 300 yards offshore.

Perfect, we would arrive just before she did. Unfortunately, her boat stayed in the same spot for three more hours.

There were two docks in Manitowoc. One was occupied by a ship under repair. The second one was occupied by a ship that had been substantially delayed in its arrival and was still unloading.

We were right. We could have played another nine and had an hour to spare!

The Epitome of "Know How"

The Swing

Among the many things I learned from my high school golf coach, Richard Yeager, was the virtue of having an uncomplicated golf swing. I distilled his advice into The Ten Commandments of Golf.

I. **Keep your eye on the ball and don't look up until you've hit it.**

II. **Bring the clubhead back close to the ground.**

III. **Turn your hips and shoulders.**

IV. **Don't let your right elbow flare out.**

V. **Don't swing from the top.**

VI. **Don't lean forward on your toes.**

VII. **Don't keep all your weight on the right side.**

VIII. **Don't let your left side collapse.**

IX. Don't rush your swing.

X. Don't think of more than one of the above when taking your swing.

Corrollary: It's best to comply with these commandments by not thinking about *any* of them when taking your swing.

I still use this list. It has some nice features. The commandments are simple and can easily be recalled and recited. The list also seems to have just the right number of commandments for the seriously committed golfer.

Following these commandments does not result in a flawless swing, but it does promise to get the ball off the ground and minimize slices, duck hooks, heels, and shanks.

Over the years I've had three basic problems with these commandments: *First,* often I comply with the Tenth Commandment by violating several other commandments. *Second,* when I violate the Tenth Commandment, I usually have a mind–body problem that results in my violating several other commandments. *Third,* even when I do think of just the right number of commandments at just the right time, I am still frequently afflicted with a mind–body problem.

Still, the commandments are useful. When things go wrong, I can usually figure out what has gone wrong. This enables me eventually to make a correction—even if it never lasts.

The really terrific thing about The Ten Commandments is that they make it unnecessary to think about the 100 or so "*How To Improve Your Swing*" theories. If I could only ever master just The Ten Commandments, I'd be satisfied. I'd certainly be a much better golfer than I am right now. When it comes to theories I find it hard to think beyond The Ten Commandments. So, if anyone ever asks me for advice, that's what they get.

That's what I tried to pass on to my friend Dick Pulaski when I introduced him to golf in the mid-1960s. It worked all right at first, but then he started getting new ideas about the swing. Each time we got together, he wanted to discuss his latest theory with me.

"All those theories just make things too complicated," I'd say. But I couldn't persuade Dick. One day it occurred to me that a classic Walter Hagen story might convince him. "Dick," I said, "there's an old story that Walter Hagen used to unnerve his opponents with by asking them whether they inhale or exhale on the downswing. Never having thought about it, they'd get confused and lose their concentration."

A couple of weeks later Dick called me to join him in a round of golf with two other friends. He said he had something to show me, but that he didn't want to tell me about it over the phone.

"Well, what do you have to show me," I asked as I met him at the course.

"You have to wait until I hit my first shot," he answered. "Then you'll see."

I watched closely as Dick addressed his ball on the first tee. His basic address and grip looked the same. But as he drew the club back, he emitted a strange sound: "B-a-a-a-r-r-r...." As he started his downswing he shouted, "R-o-o-o-mph!"

I looked in disbelief at our playing partners. Trying to hold back their laughter, they said Dick had been baaarrr-rooomphing for the past two weeks.

"I figured it out," Dick said.

"Figured out *what*?" I asked.

"Walter Hagen's question. You exhale on the *down*swing. I've even improved on it. It's like karate!"

Finally, more than 30 years after I introduced Dick to golf, he paid me an unexpected compliment. "You know," he said, "I never really appreciated how good your swing is. I've learned over the years that it's really a fundamentally sound swing." He went on to describe some of its features in theoretical terms I didn't follow very well.

"Well, like I've always tried to tell you," I said, "I just try to keep it uncomplicated."

If only it weren't so *difficult* to keep it that way when I actually swing at the ball!

Postscript: I read this little story to Dick. He paused for a moment and then commented, “You know, I think it’s even better when you exhale during the whole swing.”

Points to Ponder

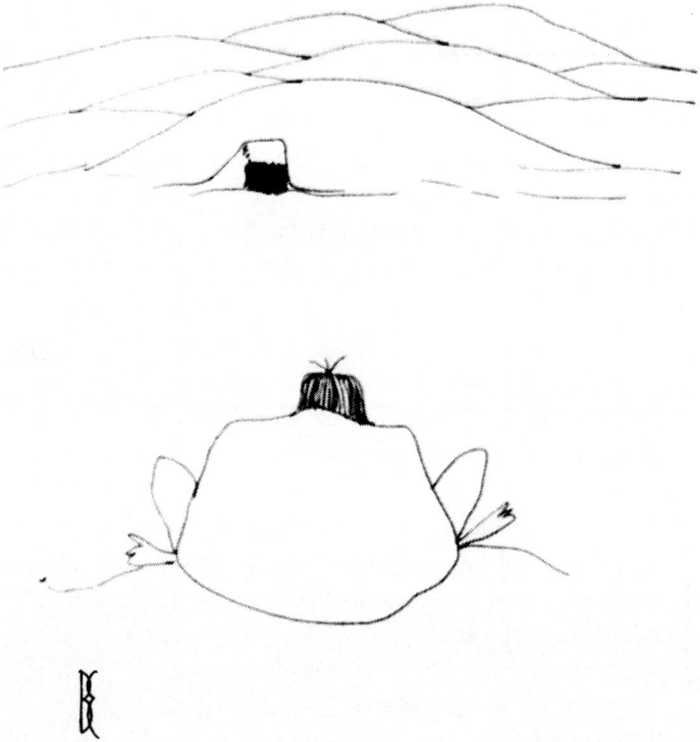

Tennis, Anyone?

One of the attractions of joining Western Michigan University's Department of Philosophy in the late 1960s was that so many faculty enjoyed playing sports together. In winter it was basketball in WMU's recreation center, where we regularly took on students in half-court games. In spring, summer, and fall it was golf. For $75 we could play an unlimited number of rounds at Milham Park, one of the finest municipal courses in the state.

However, it wasn't long before Dale Westphal discovered that we could also join Battle Creek's Bedford Valley for $75. Battle Creek residents had to pay $225, presumably because they could be expected to play more often than those who lived more than 25 miles away.

It probably hadn't occurred to the owners that four philosophers from Kalamazoo had enough time on their hands in the summer to travel 45 minutes from Kalamazoo to play golf all day several times a week. But this did occur to Dale, Dick Pulaski, Don Milton, and me.

Three-time host of the Michigan Open, Bedford Valley was wonderful—long, demanding, and beautiful. Upon arriving early in the morning, it was difficult to leave. So one day we didn't, at least not until we played 45 holes. If we were going to spend an hour-and-a-half traveling over and back, we wanted to make sure we put in a full day's work. Besides, we had an obligation to get our money's worth!

It didn't take my wife Millie long to make clear that she had a stake in this venture as well. "Did you have a good time today?" she asked.

"Yeah, we sure did."

"Well, that's great. Let's see, you were gone ten hours. So, I guess I get ten hours to do what I want to do tomorrow. You and our two-year old son should have a lot of fun together."

A quick lesson in Fairness 101! Of course Millie should have ten hours if I do. "Hmm," I calculated, "I have to play golf at least twice a week to be on top of my game. Once a week just isn't enough to be sharp. If I go on these ventures twice a week, that's 20 hours for me and 20 hours for Millie. And if I want to go a third time with the guys?" How would I find time (or energy) to work on my research? How would Millie and I find time to do anything together? What had I gotten myself into?

The next day I told my pals I wouldn't be joining them at the golf course; in fact, I was going to cut back my golfing time considerably. "I need time to work on my research—I'm writing a paper," I announced.

"Why would you want to do something like that rather than play golf?" they asked.

Part of the answer was I thought that, in addition to teaching, I should be doing research; and summers afforded me the time to do this. However, the deeper truth was that Millie had made me realize that satisfying my golfing appetite would come only at the cost of not bearing my fair share of parenting burdens. Millie wasn't really interested in having ten hours to play for every ten hours I spent on the golf course. She simply wanted me to acknowledge that ten hours is a very long stretch of time to spend alone with a two-year old, especially while one's partner is playing in the sunshine.

So, for the next 18 years I virtually gave up golf. Tennis would do: less time, more exercise, and more family togetherness. Scott was two. Susan would come along a year later. As I was to learn, parenting is a full time job—not only in the pre-school years, but even through the high school years.

I even persuaded myself that I was no longer in the grip of golf. I played occasional rounds over the years; but, I thought, I could take it or leave it. In the fall of 1987, with Susan and Scott both in college, we moved out west of Kalamazoo to live closer to Millie's place of work in Paw Paw. She had commuted from

Kalamazoo the past few years; now it was my turn. I discovered that we had moved to within three miles of Lake Cora Golf Course, a course I had played once before.

My recollection was that Lake Cora wasn't much of a golf course, but I hadn't played it in more than two decades. Maybe it had changed over the years? Curious, late that fall I took a little drive over to take a look. Indeed, it had changed. Now it had eighteen holes instead of just nine. I wondered if I'd remember the old holes and I wondered what the additional nine were like. So I tried it out. Not bad, I thought. Maybe next spring I'll buy a membership. After all, I'll be on sabbatical leave, my tennis buddies are 25 miles away in Kalamazoo, and I'll need some exercise....

There it was. One little taste was enough—the smell of freshly cut grass, the thrill of finding the "sweet spot" on the face of the club, the sense of having entered an entirely different world—where, for a little while, everything that mattered was right there.

That winter I cleaned my golf clubs for the first time in 18 years, and I began reminiscing about my youthful adventures in golf. Soon I was writing little stories, *Golf Lessons*. Hooked again.

St. Andrews

In the spring of 1975 Millie, Scott, Susan, and I paid our first visit to Scotland. We visited the torture chamber of the castle on the Isle of Skye where Bonnie Prince Charlie took refuge. We stopped at Loch Ness to see if the kids could spot the monster. We visited the ruins of old castles, and climbed their narrow, spiral stairs. We had lunch at a Chinese restaurant, where five-year old Susan looked at her soup and piped up in her perfect English accent, "Is this Chinese porridge?" We went to St. Andrews so that Millie could shop for woolen goods and I could look at the oldest golf course in the world.

To my great surprise, Millie asked me if I was going to play golf at St. Andrews. "No," I replied, "I don't think so; besides, my clubs are back home in Kalamazoo.

"But couldn't you rent some clubs?"

"Probably," I said, "but the weather is lousy. Anyway, what would you and the kids do while I played?"

"I'll take care of that," Millie reassured me. "We'll find things to do. You should go play."

"No, I don't think so."

"You can't come all the way to St. Andrews and not play the oldest golf course in the world," Millie insisted.

I never thought I'd hear Millie even encourage me to play golf, let alone *insist* on it, so how could I refuse? I teed off with a St. Andrews resident and his cousin from London. The wind was blowing in from the sea so strongly that sand from the shore was blowing in our faces, making it barely possible to see where our shots were going. Nearly the entire first nine was into the cold, stinging wind.

On the second hole the St. Andrews resident said he'd had enough. He could play any day of the year. Locals, he said, pay 12 pounds a year (about $30 then) for a membership. His cousin, playing the course for the first time, said he'd been waiting too long to play the oldest course in the world to quit. So, the two of us trudged on.

I lost at least half a dozen balls in the heather on the front nine. On the back nine the wind was behind us, so much so that I drove a 300-yard hole with a mishit 2-wood. By the end of the round all that either of us could say was that we survived. We knew that virtually every gully and trap had a special name, but we'd had no desire to pause and enjoy any of the finer points of golfing history. But I could report to Millie that I had, indeed, played the old St. Andrews course, and I could thank her for granting me the opportunity of a lifetime.

Little did I know then that this would not be my last opportunity. In 1986 I attended a conference in Edinburgh. Suddenly I had the urge to take a bus trip to St. Andrews, just to take another look at the old course. I had no hope of playing it again, as I'd heard that now it was necessary to make playing reservations a year in advance.

The weather was gorgeous that early evening in July when I got off the bus. I checked into a room and quickly walked down to the course. Oddly, the course didn't seem crowded at all. I asked the starter what the chances were of my playing. "Excellent," he said, "if you're ready to play right now. You can join those two on the first tee." I quickly rented some clubs and joined two U.S. Airforce pilots who had flown a jet from their base in Spain just to play a round at St. Andrews.

In contrast to my first visit, this time the weather was idyllic. There was a mix of deep blue sky and billowy white clouds. Pleasantly warm and virtually windless, this was not the St. Andrews I remembered from 11 years before. I floated around the course, as if in golfer's heaven. As the sun prepared to set, brilliant streaks of pink crossed the sky. Although I had played only an occasional round of golf in recent years, I felt a deep affinity to the game at that moment.

This does not mean that I played particularly well. Actually, I struck the ball well, but I seemed always to hit into trouble.

Later that evening I looked at the thick guide book for the old course handed to me at the outset by the starter. It was filled with advice from Old Tom Morris, who had figured out the best strategy to use on the course. Although this advice was issued at the turn of the twentieth century, the guidebook claimed that no one had since surpassed it. As I read through the guide, I now realized why I had so consistently gotten into trouble.

Hole by hole, according to the advice of Old Tom Morris, I had hit down the wrong side of the fairway! Still, following the advice of a guidebook would have detracted from the spontaneity of the day; and now, as I was perusing the guide, I had a deeper appreciation of the names of all those hazards with which I had become acquainted.

By the time we finished our round, the gift shop was closed. So, just before getting on the bus back to Edinburgh the next morning, I returned to the course to buy a St. Andrews golf towel to take back home to Kalamazoo. The shop was nearly empty, two other customers and the clerk. As I stood behind the two customers, I heard them talking about a familiar place. They were from Portage, right next to Kalamazoo!

Gambling

For some it seems that golf and gambling go hand-in-hand. "What's the point of playing if nothing is at stake?" they ask. For me, compounding the fear of hitting a bad shot with the fear of losing money has never made much sense. Still, there have been occasions when sociability has drawn me in.

The first time was the summer of 1957 at Hickory Hill, where I became friends with Bob, another senior-to-be, from neighboring Walled Lake High School. At least once a week Bob would wait until I finished work to join me for a friendly round of golf. At some point in the round he would suggest that we match putts for money—a dime a putt. I'd say, no, I can't afford to lose. He'd say it's just a dime. I'd win the first match, and he'd insist that he should get a second chance. I'd win the second match, and he'd demand a third. I'd win the third, and he'd ask for another match. At some point I'd say enough is enough and refuse to accept his money.

I wondered if Bob could really afford to lose all that money. I knew I couldn't. The previous summer I

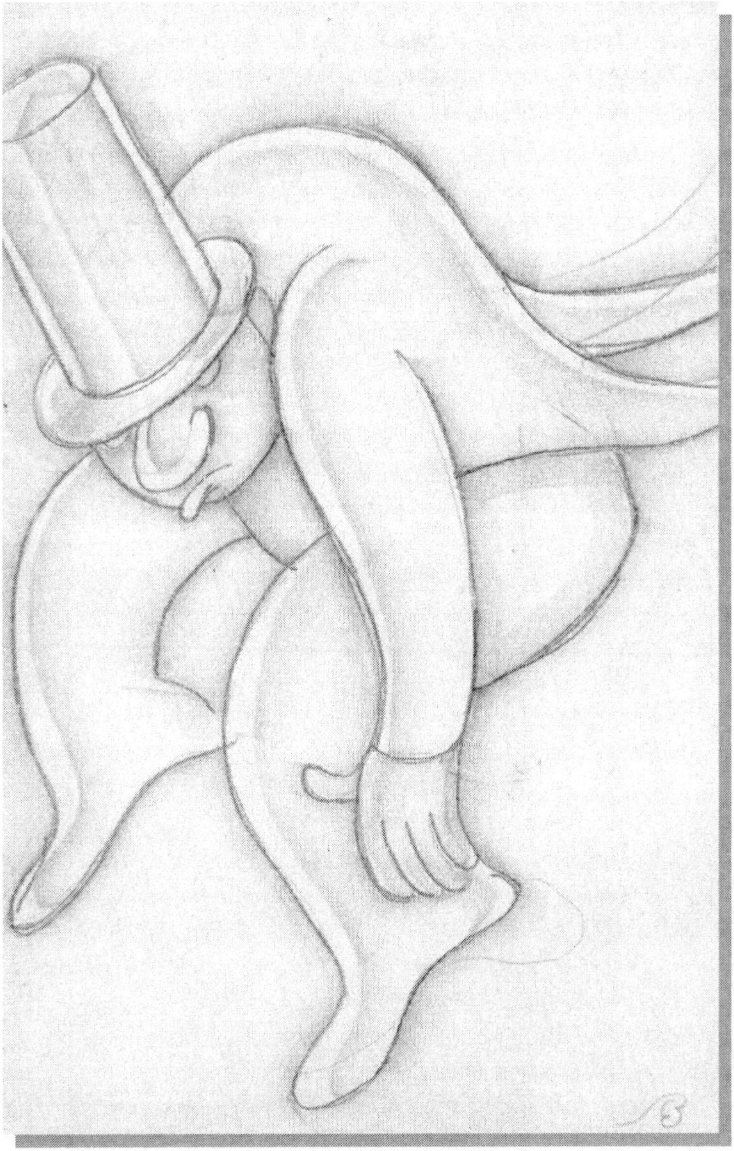

paid our several months' overdue phone bill so that our service wouldn't be discontinued. I spent most of the rest of my summer earnings on school clothes. This summer my mother was still looking for steady work. She and my father had been separated since the previous fall, and it had been even longer since he had provided us with any financial support. I was still growing, and I knew I would need to save all I could to buy school clothes again. Finally, I was trying to save $40 for a set of persimmon woods to replace the unwieldy woods I had inherited from my brother who had inherited them years before from my father. These clubs, I was sure, would be the key to improving my game for my senior year. Besides, the thought that I might lose money simply would add another obstacle to the game that, by itself, presented more than I could comfortably manage.

This resistance to gambling has stayed with me. For years I managed to avoid ever risking more than a dollar for nine holes. However, on a beautiful day in the fall of 1977 I decided to play Yale University's golf course. Millie, the kids, and I spent the 1977–78 academic year at Yale. Although I hadn't played much golf in recent years, I was intrigued by the possibility of playing an Ivy League golf course. I was disappointed to learn that I wouldn't be allowed to play unless I was the guest of a member. As I turned to leave, I heard someone say, "Our fourth couldn't make it today; you can be my guest."

As I strode up to the first tee, I learned that my three new acquaintances were Catholic priests who had hoped they'd be able to find someone to join them in their weekly high-stakes game. I had already paid $20 for greens fees, and now I was faced with the possibility of losing much more than the remaining $20 bill in my wallet. As luck would have it, my partner played extremely well, and I managed to come through with a few strong holes, too. I left the golf course with $15 more than I had when I arrived!

The following spring I was invited to join my brother Peter and his six business buddies for their annual spring golfing trip. I would take the place of someone who couldn't make it this time. Our budget for the year was tight, but Millie encouraged me to go as a March birthday present. But, I was hardly prepared for the "ground rules," which I didn't learn about until I had arrived at Jekyll Island, Georgia.

First the golf stakes were explained to me: there would be partners, with points kept for every round, and a final tally coming at the end of our three-day "tournament". Then, to my dismay, I was informed that we would be playing gin rummy when we weren't on the golf course. "But I don't know how to play," I protested. Not to worry. They'd teach me the rules and pair me up with a good partner.

Apparently I picked up the game reasonably well. My partner and I were the grand champions, but we still had to complete the golf competition. I faced the prospect of having to return all my gin rummy winnings and then some. After seventeen holes my partner and I were in second place, trailing my brother and his partner. It didn't look good for me. At least I could quietly take my brother aside and ask him if I could pay him back later.

Then it happened. Peter dribbled his drive off the tee. His second shot matched the first. Frustration mounting, he swung hard and duck-hooked his third shot into the swamp. The match was over, and my partner and I walked off with the grand prize.

My winnings eased the burden of the trip's expense a bit and lessened the guilt I'd been feeling at spending so much money for a frivolous few days in the sunshine, while Millie and the kids were stuck alone in frigid New England. Lest I return empty-handed, during each round of golf, I filled the pockets of my bag with the largest and most beautiful pine cones I had ever seen—a collection I hoped would please Millie.

With all this lucky success, why the continued aversion to gambling? Perhaps the fact that I grew up in financial insecurity had something to do with it, a reluctance to risk making a bad situation worse. However, I suspect that at least indirectly, my father gets much of the credit. Late in her life, my mother told me why he had become a traveling salesman. Early in their marriage he was caught stealing petty cash from his company during the lunch hour so that he could gamble at cards. Grandpa Eddy, who worked for the same company and helped father get his job in the first place, intervened once again. He convinced his boss simply to let my father leave his job quietly rather than have him arrested. That, my mother said, was the last time my father had a regular, salaried job. However, it was not the last time he gambled. This, she added, was a lifetime affliction.

Although it wasn't until I was in my fifties that my mother told me my father had been an inveterate gambler and this was why we never knew if he'd be bringing money home at the end of the week, I suspect that she and Grandpa Eddy found subtle ways of discouraging me from following his ways. Billiard halls were nasty places, I was told as a youngster. Only much later did I learn that one of my father's favorite pastimes was gambling at billiards.

Every time we visited my grandparents, Grandpa Eddy would lecture my father and older brother about the value of a job with regular pay as distinct from the uncertainties my father faced trying to sell encyclopedias, cemetery lots, aluminum windows and siding, fire extinguishers, or pots and pans to people who either had no interest in such products or couldn't afford them. And it was Grandpa Eddy who let me, as a little tyke, accompany him to the bank as he added a few hard-earned dollars to his savings. In contrast, my parents seemed to regard money as a taboo subject around my brother and me.

So, how could I risk losing in a flash money that, however little, Grandpa Eddy would say I'd "earned the hard way"?

Coaching

In between basketball seasons in high school, I liked to shoot hoops at home. Dribbling around the tire ruts in our dirt driveway was tough, so I concentrated on my jump shot. To keep things interesting, I imagined that I was playing in the state championship, making shot after shot. Of course, I had to take the final shot—make it and we win; miss it and we lose. If we lost, I'd start over, only this time I was the coach, and my imaginary son made shot after shot before having the final, decisive shot in his hands.

My playing in the state championship was pure fantasy. Our high school team lost nearly all of its games, and I was a regular bench rider in them. That's probably why I shifted to coaching my imaginary son. That was fantasy, too, but who knew what the distant future might hold?

Why didn't I coach my imaginary daughter? Probably because girls didn't play basketball at Milford High School or anywhere else that I knew about when I was a teenager. (Thirty years later I was surprised see a picture of my Great Aunt Aurelia holding a basketball, surrounded by her teammates on her girls' high school basketball team in Dubuque, Iowa.)

I didn't fantasize about coaching golf. That may be because I actually experienced a modicum of success on my high school and college golf teams. I just played.

I did ask my high school and college golf coaches what kind of compensation they received for coaching. Very little, they told me, except for free golf. So when Wes Dykstra, my first philosophy professor, called to ask me if I'd like to return to Alma to teach for a while, I had to ask him, "Do you think Coach Smith would be willing let me help coach the golf team?"

Actually, it was too soon for me to start teaching philosophy full time. I hadn't completed my graduate work yet, and I thought it unwise to leave Wisconsin without my doctoral degree. But when I heard that Coach Smith would have considered letting me help out coaching, I felt a twinge of regret, a lost opportunity for free golf.

The next year I took a half-time teaching job in Manitowoc, which was part of the Center System of the University of Wisconsin. I had finished taking classes, and I could write my dissertation when I wasn't teaching. Then I heard about the exclusive Black River Country Club which, for some reason, allowed the Manitowoc center golf team to practice and host golf matches there.

I quickly came up with the idea of asking Lyle Gorder, golf coach and geography instructor, if he could use some help. To my surprise he said he'd be delighted to have me take over as coach. He could use the time. Besides, he said, he actually knew very little about golf and had never been able to offer any help to the players.

So, in the spring of 1966, I became a golf coach. My first task was to offer players rides to the Black River Country Club so that I'd be sure to have at least one team member as a playing partner. I was quite sure that the country club would take a dubious view of a coach who showed up to play without anyone to coach. My second task was to coax one of my students to play in the league championship. Jim never joined us in any of the practices, but I'd heard that he was an excellent golfer.

Fortunately, Jim agreed to play in the championship. He showed up at the last minute, claiming that he had a hangover from the previous evening's activities. He quickly downed a cup of coffee and hit his first drive of the spring. He ended up with the lowest score of the day, a 69. The other players did well enough that we finished second in the league.

My colleagues congratulated me on a successful first season of coaching. But what had *I* done? I told my players that I'd give them any golfing tips I could—if only they'd ask—but they never did. I didn't make this offer to Jim. I was hoping he'd make it to practice some time so that I might see what I could learn from him, but he never practiced. Some coaching! Still, the golf was free, and the Black River Country Club was splendid.

Ten years later I took our eight-year old son, Scott, to an organizational meeting for youth soccer in Kalamazoo. As Scott and I walked in a few minutes late, I heard my friend Ron Crowell pleading to the large group of players and parents, "We really need some of you to volunteer to coach. We expected about 150 players this first year, but it looks like we have 300. There's Mike. Mike, you'll coach, won't you?"

I knew very little about soccer, but very few of the other parents did either. Before the evening was out, I agreed to help coach a team of 15 boys. The team won all of its games that year. In fact, it was nearly three years before Scott played in a losing game. But I discovered that winning games was not what coaching youth soccer was all about.

Part of the philosophy of the American Youth Soccer Organization (AYSO) is that, "everyone plays." I found myself taking this very seriously, no doubt recalling my basketball bench riding days. Any player who practiced was to play at least half of the game. I took this a step further. I worked out elaborate line-ups in which no one played the entire game, no matter how good they were, and no one played the same position for the entire time he was in the game. As many players as possible played three of the four quarters. As the game progressed, I talked with the parents—

calming them down when they were angered by the calls of the referees—urging them not to shout at their kids when they made mistakes. This was a game for the kids, not the parents, and not the coaches.

Soon our daughter Susan was playing soccer, too. So I coached two soccer teams. As Scott moved into his teens, he began to have coaches who actually knew something about the finer points of the game. Susan also was to have the benefit of more knowledgeable coaches during the four years she played on her high school team, as well as two years in college.

For me, the joy in coaching was seeing the players grow, not only in individual skills but in their ability to work together as a team. As I coached I sometimes wished that I'd had the opportunity to play soccer as a youngster. But, unlike my fantasy basketball coaching and my brief tenure as a golf coach, coaching soccer had nothing to do with *my* playing soccer in reality or fantasy. Instead, I had the good fortune of finally obtaining a glimpse of what it really means to be a coach.

Should Have

One of my most important assets in high school was my imagination. Staying awake for an entire class period sometimes took a bit of ingenuity. I drew sketches of golf courses—courses so filled with trees, traps, water, hills, and other hazards that they were virtually unplayable.

I also rehashed my most recent rounds of golf, thinking of all the unnecessary shots I took, what should have happened if only I had done this or that instead. If nothing else, golf is a game of *should have's*. Perhaps no one is more adept at discussing what should have happened than a frustrated golfer.

Years later I learned an important lesson from Snoopy, Charlie Brown's dog. This was thanks to our daughter Susan, then six. During dinner Susan kept getting up from the table and running around the house. Each time I remonstrated, "Sit down, Susan—and I *mean* it!"

Sensing I was on the verge of taking more drastic action, Susan retorted, "Unfortunately...."

"Unfortunately?!" I interrupted.

"Unfortunately, we're not playing 'I mean it' today."

As my exasperation melted into laughter, she added, "Would you like me to explain where I got that idea?" She explained that her friend Karen's lunch box had a *Peanuts* strip in which Snoopy the dog is having a miserable day on the tennis court. After each mistake he complains, "I should have done this" or "I should have done that." Finally, he concludes, "Unfortunately, we weren't playing 'should have' today."

A wise lesson to bear in mind as frustration rises to a boil on the links or in one's imagination.

False Pride?

As I size up my second shot on the tenth hole at West Shore Golf Club, I worry about the tree nearly blocking the most direct route to the flag. After all, I have already pulled my drive to the left. I wonder if I can count on the right to left breeze bringing my ball back to the left if I aim at the right side of the green. Finally, I deliberate about which club to use from 165 yards out, but somewhat downhill. Hitting from the rough, the ball might have some extra roll. Is it possible a 7-iron might roll over the green? Might I fall short with an eight? I feel strong, perhaps even a bit macho, so an 8-iron it is.

My brother Peter and I watch the ball rise high in the air, float toward the right side of the green, and gently curve left toward the flag. Dead on the pin—at last sight—but, in the bright morning haze, neither of us see the ball land.

We approach the green, with no ball in view. Someone on the neighboring hole shouts, "Did you see what happened to that ball?" We shake our heads. "It dropped in the hole!" An eagle 2! I let out a whoop, feel a real sense of accomplishment, and a surge of pride.

Now consider two 165-yard shots: one goes in the hole; the other rolls an inch wide of the hole, ending up six feet away. The one that goes in is, for me, the shot of a lifetime, the longest shot I've ever put in the hole. In more than four decades of golf, despite many close calls, I've never had a hole-in-one, and until now I'd never had a shot drop from more than 80 yards. Yet, I've hit any number of near misses. Just what is the difference? More to the point, what did *I do* that accounts for the difference?

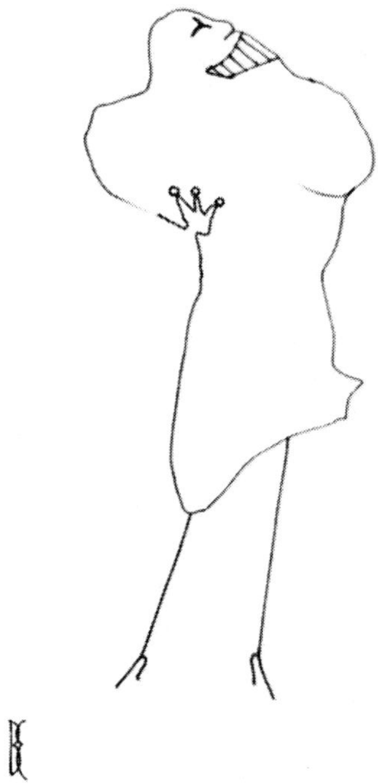

The Adoration That We All Love

Answer: nothing at all. From such a distance both shots are equally skillful. Yet, I felt a surge of pride in the shot of a lifetime that I've never felt in those near misses. Suppose I had made a few holes-in-one over the years. Would that mean that I would be a better, more skillful golfer? Not at all, only a luckier one.

Still, the aim of the game is to get the lowest score one can. A skillful, lucky shot comes closer to satisfying that aim than a skillful, unlucky one. So why not feel a little extra pride? After all, it won't last any longer than it takes to hit the next unskillful shot.

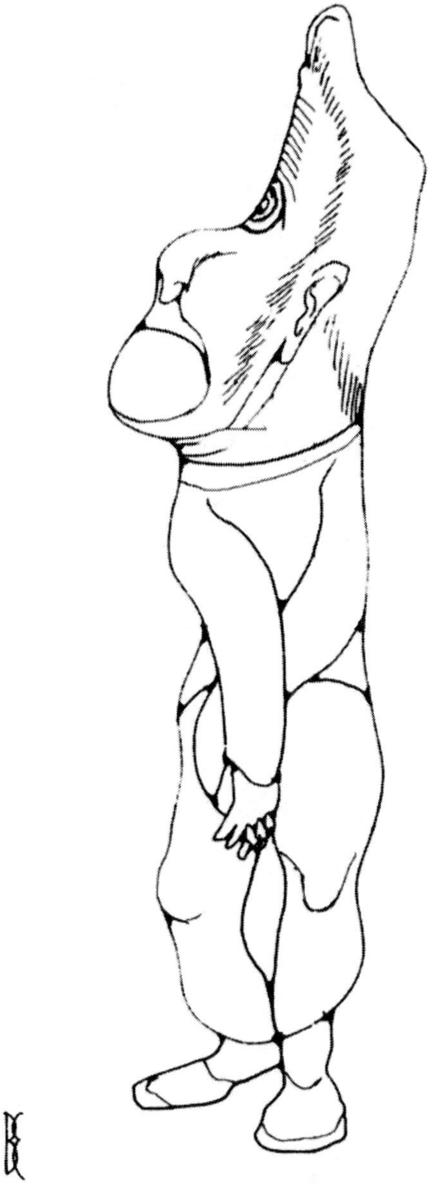

Cliff Walking

I've never thought much of the idea that "thinking it's so, makes it so," except in golf and cliff walking. Thinking the moon is made of green cheese doesn't make it so. But thinking I'm going to hit a smothered hook can make it so—or thinking I'm going to dub a drive or hit a shank or skull a wedge or miss a putt or whatever disastrous shot I imagine just before hitting it.

Golfing is like cliff walking. William James talks about cliff walking in his famous essay, "The Will to Believe." He points out that *believing* we can keep our balance while walking along a precipice is essential to being able to. More to the point, *wondering* if we can is a ticket to disaster. Even the slightest seed of doubt can upset one's balance. Each step is very much like all the others. We just put one foot in front of the other and effortlessly move forward—until, for whatever reason, we wonder how (and eventually, *whether*) such a feat is possible. We teeter a bit, and....

As for golf, in my case, it goes something like this. Three consecutive pars make me begin to appreciate how well I'm doing. This reminds me of what a wonderfully simple thing a good golf swing is. This, in turn, raises a doubt. I know from previous experience that, sooner or later, disaster will strike. How can I be doing so well *now*? As my next drive dribbles off the tee, duck hooks, or fades into oblivion, I reflect: "That swing felt just like the others, but look at the results. It's amazing how just the slightest alteration can totally mess up a shot." The mood shift is complete after my next flub. I now wonder how it is possible *ever* to hit the ball well.

I may be in the grip of this mood for some time or I may be suddenly transformed by somehow hitting another good shot. This transformation, however, is seldom negotiated through deliberation. Well, then, how *is* it accomplished?

I'm tempted to say that, when hitting a golf ball, one must concentrate totally on *now*. Banish thoughts of what has already happened; it cannot be changed. Banish thoughts of what *might* happen later; it will take care of itself. Focus solely on the task at hand—this shot, this moment, *now*. What could be simpler? One shot at a time, unselfconsciously conscious, one confident step at a time...on the edge of a precipice....

Being and Time

The most important moment in golf is *now*. Everything else is inconsequential until the score is added up. Unfortunately, *now* is very elusive for nearly every golfer. Keeping score nicely illustrates this. Consider these thoughts:

> "Since I flubbed my drive, I'll really have to crunch my next shot if I'm going to par this hole."
>
> "Since I flubbed my drive, I need to make sure I don't try to crunch my next shot. Two flubs and I'll get at least a double bogie."
>
> "All I have to do to break 80 is stay out of the trees on the last whole."
>
> "I can't believe I triple bogied that par 3. I'm really going to have to press now."
>
> "If I land in the trap, it'll be at least a double bogie."

> "Only three holes to go—all easy. I'll break 80 for sure."
>
> "All I have to do to break 80 is sink this four-foot putt."

The numbers don't matter. Some golfers are distracted by thoughts of birdies and sub-par rounds. Some would settle for bogies and scores under 90. Others despair at the thought of shooting over 100. The point is this. Each of these thoughts evades *now*. The past and the future intrude. Such intrusions invite disaster.

Richard Yeager, my high school golf coach, was right. Concentrate on one shot at a time. Think about your score as little as possible. You don't have to think about how many shots you've taken while you're playing a hole. Finish the hole, then recall how many shots you took, write down the number on the scorecard, then forget about that hole and concentrate on the next shot. When you're finished, add up the total. Then, and only then, you may muse about "what could have been," "should have been," "would have been if only…," and the like. Just hit the ball. Let the score take care of itself.

"It's fine in theory, but will it work in practice?" asked the great eighteenth century German philosopher, Immanuel Kant. (He was actually talking about something a bit more abstract than scorekeeping in golf.) Well, it *could* work in practice, but it seldom does for me—at least, not for an entire round.

But even concentrating on just one shot at a time often evades the *now*. What matters is *how* one concentrates. Looking apprehensively at the woods, water, rough, or sand trap just before hitting nearly guarantees failure, even if—or perhaps, especially if—one is concentrating only on *this* shot.

So, how does one arrive at the *now*, and what is it anyway? It's much easier to tell how one doesn't arrive at the *now*. And I find it impossible to explain what it is. I'm afraid what I have to say about all of this will seem metaphysical, obscure, or both. It is really a matter of *being* and *time* (with apologies to Heidegger). One must *be* a certain way. One must be absorbed in *this* moment. However, deliberately trying to *be* in this way typically is the wrong way to get there.

Golfers (and athletes generally) who are playing exceptionally well are sometimes said to be "unconscious." This is a misnomer. They are quite conscious, but their attention is focused away from themselves; they are not *self*-conscious. The *now* in golf is something like *deja vu*. One cannot decide to experience it. When we are in its grip, we are focused on something else. When we become aware of its presence, it goes "poof" and ceases to *be*.

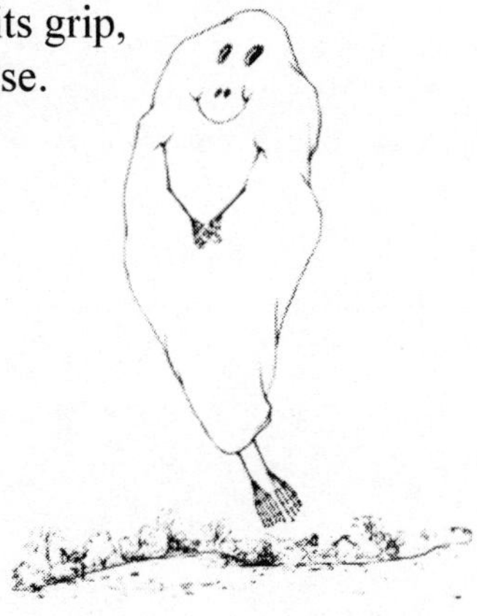

Witnessing

You'd think that more than 50 years of playing golf would yield at least one hole-in-one. No such luck. I've come close—very close. One inch. Well, maybe two inches, but only because it bounced back from the hose that was so thoughtlessly placed across the hole. Well, I didn't actually *see* it bounce back. After all, it's hard to see just what a little white ball is up to when it's 140 yards away. But as anyone could plainly see, the ball blazed a trail through the early morning dew right up to the edge of the hole.

Unfortunately, none of this really matters. No one else was there to witness it, and *real* holes-in-one require witnesses. In fact, all *real* golf scores are supposed to have witnesses. That's why scorecards always have a place marked, "Witness." I guess no one trusts golfers by themselves.

That's too bad, because I play a lot of golf by myself. That's when I work on my virtues, especially the virtue of generosity. Sometimes I'm generous to a fault. For example, if I'm in a hurry, I use my Gimmee Rule. I know I can make any putt within, say, four or five feet from the hole. So, why putt it? Of course, if I never practice such putts I might lose my touch. Sometimes I putt them to keep sharp. Occasionally I miss—but only after I've already applied my Gimmee Rule, and golf rules are not to be taken lightly. Besides, since no one is watching, none of this *really* counts anyway.

You might say that playing alone is just practicing, preparing for the *real* thing—playing with others and *really* keeping score. I suppose there's more to it than this. Once in a while I engage in "golf talk":

> "Do you play golf, Mike?" an acquaintance may ask.
>
> "Quite a bit."
>
> "What's your handicap?"
>
> "My swing."
>
> "Come on, be serious. What do you shoot?"
>
> "Well, since I usually play alone, I don't really keep score."
>
> "Don't give me that. If you're any kind of golfer, you know what you shoot. What's the matter, can't count that high?"
>
> "Right, wise guy. What do you shoot?"

"Oh, usually one or two over."

I know a bluff when I hear one. This guy probably has a Gimmee Rule a mile long. He's the same guy who tells me he hits the ball 275 yards on a rainy day. He presses on, "I shot a 38 on the backside of TeeTorn the other day, with 40-mile-an-hour winds! And you should have seen my drive on seventeen."

What can I say? That I once shot a 41 there without my Gimmee Rule? He's not going to tell me about his Gimmee Rule so why should I tell him about mine? "That's pretty good. My best score on that side is 37, but I have to admit the weather was perfect."

Still, this doesn't really explain why I need my Gimmee Rule. Why can't I just exchange whoppers with others, but tell myself the truth?

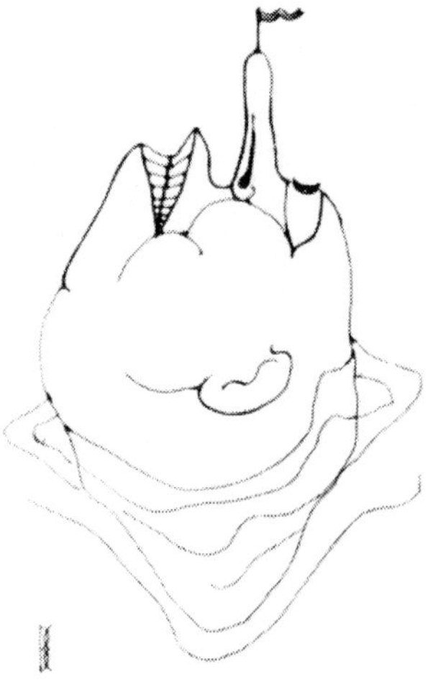

Yogi

New York Yankee hall-of-famer Yogi Berra is famous for saying of baseball games, "It ain't over 'til it's over." The same might be said of golf.

As we stood on the ninth tee at Grosse Ile's West Shore Golf Club, my brother Peter commented, "This hole is my nemesis. I've been playing it all summer, and I've never gotten less than a 6." I looked down the fairway toward the green. About 400 yards, no special twists or turns, just a couple of traps around the green. What could be so troublesome for him about this hole?

"Maybe this is the day," I replied.

After two shots, Peter was a pitching wedge from the green. He took aim and fired his ball into the left trap. "See," he grumbled, "I can never get less than 6."

"Sure you can," I smilingly reassured him, "Just hit a spectacular shot from the trap to 18 inches from the hole." Peter's shot rose gently over the yawning face of the trap, settled nicely onto the middle of the green, and rolled confidently within 18" of the cup. Good-bye nemesis.

Peter stood over his putt. Fifty yards away another golfer leaned toward the door of the club's refreshment house to order a drink. As Peter drew his putter back the golfer shouted, "Bud Light!" The ball rolled gently past the hole. Yogi's right.

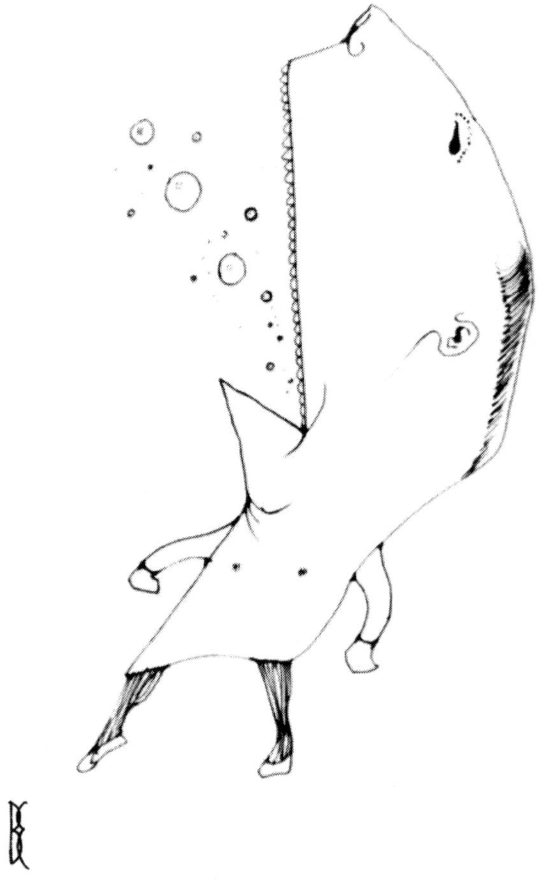

Paw Paw

The Right Stuff

Some years ago I noticed that grooves in the grip of my 9-iron had worn through to the metal shaft, the result of 28 years of index fingers rubbing against that grip. I ran my hands over the grips of my other irons. *Very* smooth, as smooth as tires with 120,000 miles on them. All but my 2-iron, that is. Its grip was almost like new. I hadn't had the nerve to hit more than half a dozen shots with that club in 28 years. "These are *grips*?" I thought.

No wonder my clubface kept turning on impact! New grips would take care of those spraying, straying shots. You have to have the *right stuff.*

The new grips helped for awhile, after they stopped feeling like they were made for grass whips. But old habits die hard. Soon I figured out how I used to hit duck hooks, heels, and shanks before my 28-year old grips had left their infancy.

Fortunately, it wasn't too serious. Over the years I've developed a motto: If you're going to laugh about it sooner or later, it might as well be sooner. It works pretty well for me about 95 percent of the time, except for golf, but even there it's up to about 25 percent and still rising. The problem is that it's a little distracting when you're ready to hit your next shot and you're still laughing about how you got stymied by that pine tree.

Besides, really serious-minded golfers (the vast majority) think you're crazy. And they get really irritated when you forget that the shot you're laughing at is *theirs*, not yours. So, if you don't want to play alone all the time, 35 percent is probably about as high as you should go.

Actually, it's hard to talk about percentages these days. Athletes are always talking about how they gave 120 percent. It's really confusing when they talk about their injuries, "I'm only about 60 percent recovered. Doc says I can't play 'til I'm 80 percent, but I'll give it 120 percent then."

Monetary inflation has done wonders to our psyches. It's even infected my student requests for letters of recommendation:

> **Student**: Professor Pritchard, will you write a letter of recommendation for me?
>
> **Prof. Pritchard**: Only if you want me to tell the truth, the whole truth, and nothing but the truth.

Student: No, I want *more* than that.

I normally resist such nonsense. But one day, while in the grip of my dentist, the subject turned to sweetspots. It's hard to ask questions with a drill in your mouth. So I could only listen while he talked on about power, sweetspots, and *'ping-imitations*.' Was he talking about *my* teeth? Surely I didn't need a fake tooth, did I? I'll quit eating so many sweets—really!

"Of course you can still eat sweets, Mike," he reassured me as I rinsed out my mouth. "I'm talking about *club*faces, not *your* face. You did ask me how my golf game was a few minutes ago, didn't you?"

I should have been able to figure it out. My dentist was first and foremost a golfer. He worked patients in between golf trips. He had been telling me about the set of "Ping imitations" he bought his son-in-law for Christmas. "Sweet spot as wide as your mouth," he'd said. *This* I had to see.

My mouth watered when I saw those new clubs. They looked like the real thing—authentic, like those old toy six-shooters I always preferred. The clubfaces even looked more like pistol grips than my old Gormans. Imagine drawing one of those long-barrelled weapons out of my golf bag, taking a shot, then jamming it back in before the smoke cleared!

It was clear that I *had* to have those clubs, but I still needed a *justification*—the bane of my philosophical existence. How could I spend $200 on something so frivolous? Well, my Gormans were now nearly 30 years old. Some of my friends had gone through several sets of clubs during that period, maybe even six sets; that's at least $1200 or $40 a year. I'm talking about less than $7 a year—so what if I've been saving it all up for *now*.

Millie will understand. I've sacrificed $7 worth of frivolity every year for the last *30* years. Why, she's spent more on shoes in the last five years than I have on golf clubs *and* shoes in the last 30! Besides I just got $200 for a lecture this week, and I didn't even know I was giving it until four days ago. Strike while the iron's hot!

But what about that *big* sweet spot? What would Sam Snead say? He used to hit stones with a stick. What kind of sweet spot did he need? Tommy Armour? He tried to keep the game simple, but would he approve of getting rid of duck hooks and slices without actually improving your swing? What about Coach Yeager? Would he approve of my finally getting away with swinging too hard? And how about Baldie?

Purist! Hadn't I already compromised in tennis? Admittedly, I was a little sneaky about that. First, I went for the slightly oversized Head Edge, but finally I went for the whole thing—the Prince! Still, I didn't do it *all* at once. And, it wasn't without a little guilt.

But why should I feel guilty? This is the age of inflation. Almost no one's as good as they look, least of all those Young Male Golfers who never had to hit with Gormans. Who am I to look as good as I am when everyone else looks better?

So I bought those clubs with a sweet spot wider than my mouth. My birthday was the clincher. I bought them for my forty-eighth birthday. Surely no one else would buy me such a present. Others might deny me the pleasure, but why should *I* add to my misery?

I tried out my new clubs. For the first time I understood what it meant to hit a ball with a "feathery touch". That expression mystified me for years. I tested out the full range of the sweet spot. It goes from heel to toe. Outside that range only two things can happen—a whiff or a shank. Oh, yes, shanks are still possible, but only with considerable effort.

It's perfectly clear to me now. You just need to have the *right stuff*.

Postscript: Writing some years later, much has happened since purchasing my new irons. Now it's the metal woods—with huge, titanium heads and bubble shafts that make the ball go straighter and, best of all, *farther*. They are rather pricey, but even the youngsters use them. So how can I resist?

The Green Monster

For most sports fans, "Green Monster" conjures up memories of line drives off Fenway Park's famous green wall. But that's baseball. I want to talk about golf's Green Monster.

"Try this," said my golfing buddy, Al. He handed me a metal driver with an oversized head.

"What's this? The Green Monster?" I asked.

"Never mind," Al replied. "Just try it. I can't handle it myself, but I think you might like it."

After a few swings, the Green Monster and I developed a very nice relationship. In return for swinging it gently, this oversized gem rewarded me with monster drives. It seemed that, with the least effort, my drives were going 15 to 20 yards farther than ever before—and straighter.

"Try it out for a while," offered Al. "I never use it, and I like to see you hit with it." For the next few weeks I continued using the Green Monster. It seldom disappointed me. Finally Al said, "Keep it, Mike. It's yours."

"I can't do that, Al. This is a really expensive club."

"Keep it. I've got more clubs than I know what to do with."

"Well, how about if I just keep on borrowing it for a while?"

"Fine, fine, 'borrow' it—forever, as far as I'm concerned."

I did borrow it for a while longer. But then I began thinking that I should have one of my own, a brand new one, so off I went to a golf shop. Although no Green Monsters were available, there was no dearth of oversized, overpriced substitutes. Narrowing my choice to three, I ventured out to the driving range. One club seemed distinctly superior to the other two. It seemed to have that Green Monster feel, with results to match.

Later that day I returned the Green Monster to Al. "Thanks a lot for letting me use it; it inspired me to invest in one of my own."

After briefly inspecting my new club, Al looked at me in disbelief, grumbling, "Looks nice, but it's no Green Monster—and it's not free either!"

Over the next several weeks I set out to prove to Al that I had made no mistake. I'd show him that my club matched the Green Monster. Each time I hit an impressive drive, Al would chortle, "Good thing you didn't hit that with the Green Monster—it'd be on the green."

As the weeks went by, I was sure Al would let up. But he didn't. Finally, after hitting what I thought was an especially impressive drive, I turned to Al, "All right. Hand me the Green Monster and I'll prove to you once and for all that I didn't make a mistake buying my club!"

Grinning, Al handed me the Green Monster. As I took a practice swing, I had to admit that the old club had a special feel to it. But so, I thought, did my new one. I swung easily at the ball. Whaaack!!! The ball snapped off the clubhead with stunning authority. I watched it soar down the middle of the fairway, landing a full 15 yards beyond its supposedly splendid predecessor.

Al's grin burned through the brim of my hat as, head lowered, I handed him his Green Monster.

Playing With the Pro

Aristotle says we acquire virtues through habituation—we keep doing good things until it becomes habit-forming. The same is true of vices and golf swings. Decades of swinging a golf club leaves its indelible marks, so I'm naturally a bit wary when I start to sense that someone might want to tamper with my swing. It's not that I think that my swing is so fixedly wonderful; it's that, by now, it's the only one I have—and very possibly the only one I *can* have.

It is the summer of 1995. Ernie is the teaching pro at Lake Cora Golf Course, my place of refuge nearly every evening. I know he sees me swing at the ball from time to time, but from a safe distance.

Take the other day, for example. As I strode up to my ball to hit my second shot on number three, I saw Ernie about 150 yards away. "Maybe he's watching," I thought, so I fussed over my shot a little longer than usual. Taking the club back slowly, I could feel the confidence surging through my limbs. Whack! I watched my ball arch toward the green and land some 230 yards from the point of impact. "How do you like that, Ernie?" I chortled to myself. A few moments later I ran in my putt for an eagle 3.

I'm now down to only two commandments: No. III, "Turn your hips and shoulders"; and No. X, "Don't think of more than one commandment when swinging." The rest will take care of itself, I think. As I arrived at the seventh tee, I was playing beyond myself, 1 under par. As I watched my drive veer sharply left, I realized that I had followed only one of the two commandments. I hadn't thought of more than one commandment when swinging; I hadn't thought of any. I reminded myself of No. III.

Of course, remembering No. III isn't always enough. Mind and body have to work together in golf, always a challenge. Unfortunately, my body seemed to be in a particularly disobedient mood for the rest of the nine. But the back nine would be different, I resolved.

Then Ernie reappeared. This time he was only a few yards away. "Hey, why don't you join us?" he urged, pointing to the empty seat in his electric cart.

"That's okay. I'm only going to play a few more holes."

"So are we—strap your bag on the cart!"

Suddenly I felt the full crush of 41 years of avoidance. Never in all those years had I treated myself to a professional golf lesson. A few suggestions and hints from friends. A few remonstrances from my high school and college coaches. But they were all (un)rank(ed) amateurs. I had studiously avoided golf professionals.

Maybe my friend Dick finally conceded that I had a decent golf swing, but what did *he* know? A bunch of high flying theories and whatever *I* had taught *him*. Maybe my swing has a fatal flaw—a flaw that a real pro could see in an instant from up close, a flaw so deeply ingrained that it's incurable. "I'm happy the way I am," I thought. "Trial-by-error golf is good enough for me, always has been, and always will be." Lots of trial and lots of error.

Too late! My bag is strapped to Ernie's cart. I watch Ernie's two young protégés crush their drives. I watch Ernie effortlessly hit his far and straight. I stand over my ball, mind locked in fear, and hit a horrendous slice. "Even Jack Nicklaus slices it like that sometimes," grins Ernie.

"Sure," I silently muse, "sometimes he hits slices, but not like *that* one—unless it's with his 8-iron." I then line drive my 8-iron sharply left and into the pond.

But I have an explanation for both shots. Poor hip and shoulder turn. Violation of Commandment No. III. The same shortcoming, I theorize, is responsible for either blocking to the right or pulling left.

I hit my next three drives hard, but left. "Turn the hips and shoulders," I mutter to myself. Meanwhile

I wonder, "What do you suppose Ernie sees, right up close? I *feel* like I'm turning. What do I know anyway? Theory by trial and error?"

So my worst golfing nightmare is upon me. "4 KILLER MISTAKES," screamed the September 1995 cover of *Golf Magazine*. "We analyzed 1,000,000 shots and found...," read the subtitle. Found what? How many of those killer mistakes had Ernie found in my swing? Why didn't I ever learn to really slow down my swing like Coach Yeager counseled me in high school? Was I afraid someone would see how I really swing? (A swing faster than the eye....) Was it the position of my head, my grip, my stance, my wrists, my everything?

Finally I hit a fairway wood straight down the middle on the par 5 fifteenth. "You hit a pretty good one," Ernie said. "But...but what, Ernie?" I wondered while waiting for his fatal diagnosis.

Instead, Ernie began talking about his two young protégés. "You know," he said, "those guys never listened to me when they were kids. I kept telling them not to lurch at the ball—that they'd never be consistent that way. Now that they have jobs, they can't play much. And they wonder why the game's so hard for them. They just wouldn't learn the basics."

"Oh, oh," I thought. "Now the other shoe's going to drop, spikes and all, right on my head. He's really set me up for this one." However, we finished the hole in silence. The sun had now set, and Ernie drove me to my car. "It's so bad he doesn't have the heart to tell me," I think.

As I put my clubs in the trunk, Ernie turned me and said, "You're okay. You just need to be careful with your backswing. You weren't getting a full turn. It probably felt like you were. But you weren't."

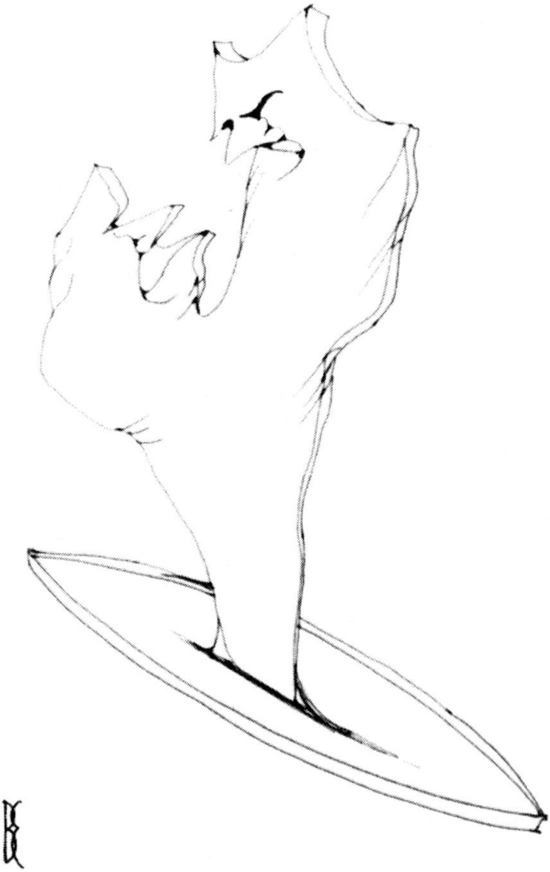

Soundbites

The TV reporter asked, "Do you think there's any connection between golf and philosophy?"

"Yes," I replied somewhat hesitantly, "I suppose there are some special connections between golf and philosophy."

This was the year that New Orleans hosted, quite coincidentally, a professional golf tournament and the annual meeting of the Central Division of the American Philosophical Association. As my wife Millie and I walked into the book exhibit room, she noted the NBC cameras and wondered why they were there. We saw Martin Benjamin, a friend and fellow philosopher from Michigan State University, walking from the cameras in our direction. "There's Martin," I said, "let's ask him if he knows."

"There's a PGA golf tournament in town right now, and the local NBC affiliate heard about our convention. They're looking for philosophers who play golf. I guess they think there could be a good story in

that. I just told them about you—they're waiting for you to come over."

Taken by surprise, I replied, "I don't know what I'd say."

"Sure you do," Millie insisted. "You've been writing all those golf stories." Nudging me in the direction of the cameras, she added, "This may be your big opportunity."

"For example?" continued the reporter.

.

My mind went blank. Then I remembered the Stoics. "Well, the Stoic philosophers advised us not to get too excited when things are going well or too down when things are going badly. That's good advice for golfers. Golf, like life, has its peaks and valleys."

"Who would be an example of a Stoic philosopher?"

After silently fumbling for a few names, I decided I wouldn't risk picking the wrong one on camera, especially not at a meeting of professional philosophers. So I feebly replied, "Well, I can't think of any particular names right now."

"Okay, let's stop the camera for a minute." Fortunately, the reporter would have time to edit his tape. I sensed that he was looking for something I hadn't quite given him. A *soundbite*. That's what he wanted. A clever little nugget in a nutshell. I shifted nervously, feeling hopelessly inadequate to the task.

After a few words of encouragement, the reporter resumed his questioning. "Do you think there's a Zen to golf?"

"I suppose there is."

"Tell us about it."

"I really don't have anything to say about it."

End of interview. I was told that the program would be on the local news at five o'clock. Luckily I had a meeting then; however, Millie watched the program. "You were on for a few seconds," she told me later that evening. "They did the peaks and valleys bit. That was nice. But they did find another philosopher, someone who gave them just the kinds of things they wanted. Just a lot of fluff—no substance. Then they closed with a golfer sinking a putt, with the reporter commenting, 'I putt, therefore, I am.'"

"How cute," I mumbled. "A clever play on Descartes's, 'I think, therefore, I am.'" But not clever enough, I mused. You can't meaningfully deny that you think, but nobody *has* to putt.

The next morning I woke up with a BC comic strip running through my head. One of the characters is carrying a large club. As he clobbers a compatriot over the head, the caption reads, "**THUNK!**" He then triumphantly walks away saying, "I **THUNK**, therefore, I am!" Imagine a golfer uttering those words after thunking his drive. What a soundbite! Where was it when I needed it?

Millie couldn't remember the name of the more resourceful philosopher on the news program. Suppressing my envy as best I could, I asked some friends if they knew who he might be. "Oh, yes," said one, "I know him well. He'll talk about anything—but it's all bull, no substance."

So, there it was again, back to soundbites. "Soundbites," I thought, "insubstantiality wrapped in a nutshell." I then consoled myself with something I once heard Michigan State philosopher and physician Howard Brody say at the beginning of one of his talks: "I'll try to put my philosophy in a nutshell. But I'm afraid that any philosophy that can be put in a nutshell ...probably belongs there."

Breckenridge

"You could *die* up here!" Jim Jaksa stood before me, shivering in the cold wind, several thousand feet above Denver. "Obviously lots of people *have* died here," I replied. "Look behind you." As Jim turned around, he was surprised to find himself facing an old cemetery not more than 50 feet away.

This was Jim's first time in the Rockies. As soon as we got into our rental car at the airport, he asked me to drive us into the mountains. We could check into our motel later. Actually, we had come to Denver to interview engineers about ethics in the workplace, but this didn't mean we couldn't have fun.

After completing our interviews we ventured back into the mountains, winding our way up to Breckenridge, a well-known resort town for skiers. But it was a golf course, not the ski slopes that attracted our attention. It was mid-summer, and neither of us had hit a golf ball 9,600 feet above sea level.

The Breckenridge golf course was surrounded by snow-capped mountains. We joined another twosome on the tee of the first hole, a 340-yard par 4. Our two new companions hit nice looking drives to within a hundred yards of the green. Jim did likewise.

Maybe they'd clobbered their first drives, but I was going to take it easy until I'd gotten used to my rental clubs and the elevation. So, I left the driver in the bag and opted instead for a light swing with my 3-wood. I was surprised to see the ball hang so long in the air as it headed in the direction of the green, finally landing on the apron of the green. I spent the rest of the afternoon trying to figure out what clubs to use. Still, hitting 8-irons from more than 200 yards out was fun, no matter how far over the green they landed.

Although the sky was bright and sunny when we teed off, we were told to be ready for fast-moving storms. If we saw one coming, we should head for the clubhouse without delay. Just before finishing the first nine, we saw large flashes of lightning in the distance. We made it to the clubhouse just in time. In a matter of minutes the storm blew through, leaving in its wake a gorgeous rainbow, both of whose ends seemed to be within the confines of the golf course. Then another equally gorgeous rainbow arched right over the first one.

"I'm going to get my camera from the car, Jim," I said excitedly. "I've never seen both ends of a rainbow before; and I've never seen a double rainbow either. I need a picture of this." I ran to the car, got my camera, pointed at the double rainbow and clicked—only to discover that I was out of film. With that, the rainbow disappeared as quickly as it appeared! Of course, there still was the testimony of two professors who had spent the last ten years teaching a course together on honesty and deception; but without a shred of evidence, who would believe us back in Michigan?

Speaking of which, as we were loading our car to leave our Breckenridge accommodations, I was told by the desk clerk that my daughter was calling from home. I took the call at the front desk and noticed him listening intently to my end of the conversation. During our stay at the hotel Jim and I had found this young man to be a sometimes annoying non-stop talker, someone seemingly incapable of keeping a thought to himself.

"Are you sure she's dead?" I asked Susan. "Right, I don't think we should tell your mother until she gets back from Chicago—she'd probably fall apart. What should we do with her? Well, why not bury her in the woods?"

For the first time in the two days we'd stayed at the hotel, the desk clerk was silent, with a horrified look on his face. Finally he burst out, "Please tell me that you weren't talking about a *person* to be buried in the woods! It *had* to have been some sort of animal."

I explained that one of our young cats, Calvin, had inexplicably died overnight. Susan had found her stretched out in rigor mortis that morning and called me to find out what to do. As we drove back to Denver,

Jim shared our amusement at what it had taken to render the desk clerk speechless, if only for a moment.

Of course, losing one's pet is not a laughing matter; and, on returning home, I got my own just desserts for finding anything amusing about the situation. I decided to call Millie in Chicago, after all. It might spoil her meeting, but it would be even worse for her to come home and find out that one of our cats had been dead for three days.

"What caused her to die?" Millie asked.

"I don't have any idea. Susan just found her lying there dead—no bleeding, just dead."

"Well, we need to find out what caused her to die. It could be something contagious. We need to protect the other four cats. Take her to the vet and have an autopsy done."

"But he's already buried," I protested, beginning to feel my stomach churning at even the thought of digging up poor Calvin.

"Take her to the vet!" insisted Millie.

I called the vet, fervently hoping that he would say that he doesn't do autopsies on buried cats. "Bring her in," said an enthusiastic vet. "I love doing autopsies and trying to solve puzzles like this."

Turning pale as I gingerly poked around for the spot where Susan said she buried Calvin, I finally located her body and placed it in a plastic bag. I dropped Calvin off on my way to work that morning, greatly relieved that I had somehow overcome my squeamishness and satisfied Millie's request.

Later that day I received a call from the vet. "Well," he said, "I've completed the autopsy. No poison and nothing else that I could tell—looks like she died from natural causes. I wouldn't worry about the other cats picking up anything from her." I thanked him for his efforts. He concluded, "Thanks for the opportunity. You can come get your cat now."

Come pick up my cat now? Unfortunately, my work wasn't finished. I had to pick up poor Calvin and bury her again!

For the Hopeists*

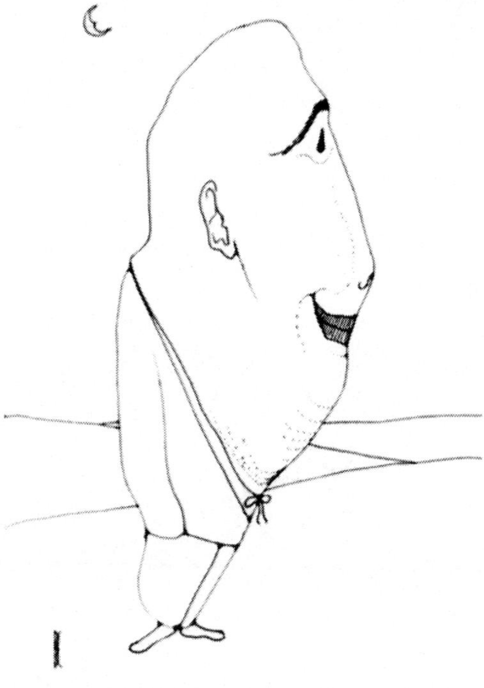

* What is a "hopeist"? I once heard William Stieg, author and illustrator of children's books, say in a TV interview that he was neither an optimist nor a pessimist. Because he couldn't honestly say that he believes the future will be better than the past, he wasn't an optimist. He wasn't a pessimist because that would work against the future being better than the past. So, he concluded, he was a hopeist—living his life with the hope that the future will be better than the past.

Zoning Out

Professor Ann Margaret Sharp read a few paragraphs of her paper, paused to take several deep breaths, and finally asked moderator Mort Morehouse if he could get her a glass of water. As she continued, her breathing became more labored. Suddenly I recognized the symptoms. I had been there many times myself. Ann was, to coin a phrase, "zoning out." After continuing her struggles a bit longer, she turned to Mort and asked him if he could take over reading her text for a while. Stunned, Mort turned to the audience and burst out, "I can't do it; I'm dyslexic!" Then he saw a familiar face in the front row. "Michael, come up here and help Ann for a while."

As I walked up to the podium, I recalled my zoning-out days and I wondered if it could happen to me now. In the sixth grade I struggled mightily when asked to read out loud in class. While reading my assigned paragraph, I began hearing my voice as if it were someone else's. The words poured smoothly out of my mouth, but I had no comprehension of what I was reading. How could I continue this way, I wondered. In fact, *where* was I? Worse, *was* I? It was as though I was vanishing—yet the sounds continued, as if on their own. I was zoning out. Fearing I would fade away entirely, I barely finished my paragraph.

For the next several months I did everything I could to prevent this disturbing experience from recurring. On reading days we took turns, going in order up and down the rows, so I counted ahead to determine which paragraph I would have to read. Occasionally, when a paragraph was especially short, Mr. Pinckney would ask the student to read a second one as well, causing me to shift quickly to the next paragraph—hoping, desperately, that it would be neither too long nor too short.

Matters came to a head when I panicked in the middle of a long paragraph and cried out that I couldn't continue. My parents and I then met with Mr. Pinckney. It was pointed out that I was very young for the sixth grade, as I had started kindergarten at age four. Perhaps I should be held back a year? At that I immediately objected, pledging to try my best to complete my paragraphs. I also promised myself that I would never again tell my parents or teachers about these terrifying moments. I would somehow figure out how to cope with them on my own.

It wasn't just in the classroom that I zoned out. It also happened the next summer while playing softball. At practice I zoned out while catching throws at first base. Fearing I could be injured, or at the very least make some embarrassing errors, I asked to be moved to right field where there would be less action.

Our first game was the next evening. The coach told me he'd stop by to take me to the game. When he pulled into our driveway, I fled to the attic, pushed open a little window, and shouted down that I didn't feel well and wouldn't be going. In truth, I was afraid of zoning out. With a little coaxing from my mother, I relented and went to the game.

I hit a home run my first time at bat. The second time I hit a grand slammer. As I floated around third base, I heard loud cheers and began zoning out. Greeted at home plate by slaps on the back and bear hugs from my teammates, I heard a voice scream out, "Leave me alone! Leave me alone!" As my teammates backed away, I burst into tears, and my panic melted into embarrassment as I realized that among the onlookers was Lois Christian, the girl I'd hoped most to impress that evening.

The fear of zoning out dogged me all the way through junior and senior high school. As an eighth grader I was nominated to run for president of the class. Somehow I found the courage to make a short speech before a filled auditorium that included both junior and senior high students. My brother Peter, a senior, suggested that beginning with a little self-effacing humor would help me relax and win over the audience in one quick move. He found a joke for me about a speaker whose knees were nervously rattling, like a milkman who couldn't keep his milk bottles from rattling as he delivered them on doorsteps. Voice shaking nervously, I banged my knees together a few times. The audience laughed—either with me or at me;

I couldn't tell which. In any case, for the next two minutes I raced through my carefully prepared set of notes on three-by-five-inch cards, bringing myself perilously close to zoning out.

I received three votes, one from the student who nominated me, the other two from a couple of loyal friends. I cast my vote with the rest of the class and voted for Jerry "Tuffy" Thompkins, the best tackler on the eighth-grade football team. My only distinction in football that year was getting knocked out trying to tackle the team's best runner. Of course, I was only twelve, and "Tuffy" was already fifteen. But he was also the most popular kid in the eighth grade.

Fortunately, we seldom had to read out loud in high school. However, basketball posed somewhat of a dilemma. Much as I wanted the coach to put me in games, I feared that I might become unhinged right there in front of hundreds of onlookers. As it turned out, I had little to worry about. For the most part, I rode the bench until the closing minutes of our games, when the outcome was no longer in doubt. So, if I needed to, as I sometimes did, I could float through the last few seconds.

Golf, however, provided me with a real opportunity to approach my problem constructively. My high school golf matches were nine holes, requiring an hour-and-a-half of concentrated effort. Occasionally I would begin to zone out, especially after hitting several good shots in a row. "How am I able to hit the ball so well, time after time?" I'd ask myself. "Can I do it this time?" I'd look down at my arms and legs, seeing them as if they were someone else's or no one's. As panic began to set in, I would hit a wayward shot or two. But I discovered that if I just kept on playing, everything eventually would return to normal. No doubt it helped to have quiet moments to myself while walking to my next shot.

Catching a ball, running around the bases or up and down a basketball floor, jumping, dribbling, passing, or shooting might pose problems; but there was nothing like a triple bogie to bring me back to reality.

This worked so well on the golf course that I elected to take a speech class my senior year. There I learned that most of my classmates were as afraid of speaking in front of others as I was, regardless of whether they'd ever zoned out.

Our teacher, Mr. Mathis, suggested that we select a few people as our special audience rather than think about everyone at once. Imagine, he said, that you are talking with, first this person, then that person, then a third, then back to the first, and so on—rather than a large, anonymous audience. This helped me keep things going, until I began to zone out. Then I tried my golf trick—just keep on talking until it passes. Even if I flubbed a line, all would soon be well.

Eventually I stopped zoning out. I became a professor, undaunted by audiences as large as 600. I found myself actually enjoying making presentations at professional meetings around the country and even around the world.

So, how hard could it be to get up before 100 other philosophers and school teachers at a national conference and read a little bit of Ann's paper? Zoning out? I couldn't remember the last time I had to deal with that. Still, I was thinking about it, imagining the irony of zoning out while trying to help a zoned-out friend. I also thought about the fact that this was my first time at the podium with my brand new bifocals. The print was tiny, the text lengthy, and the content totally unfamiliar. I soon found myself reading words without comprehension, just like in the sixth grade. Would zoning out be next? Just keep on reading. Besides, Ann said she'd take over in a couple of minutes. But she never did. I read for a full hour while she sat smiling in the front row.

"Why," I asked her later, "didn't you come up and finish your presentation?"

"You were doing such a wonderful job, Michael," she replied. "You made my paper sound so good. I was really enjoying listening to it."

After returning from the conference, I recounted this story to my mother, reminding her of my classroom difficulties in the sixth grade. "Oh, that's when," she quickly recalled, "I was afraid to leave the house. I tried to hide it from you, but maybe you sensed something was going on. It was a very difficult time for me." Mother may have been afraid to leave the house, but I do know that she went with my father and me to talk with the teacher about my problems. This must not have been easy for her. Looking back, I now recall that she didn't attend that first softball game, but she did coax me down from the attic.

Fifty-Nine...and Fading?

In March my thoughts turn to birthdays and golf. On the maternal side of my family, my grandmother, mother, daughter, and I all were born in March. In addition, my daughter-in-law Amy leads the way, March 1. Unfortunately, in February I'm not thinking of March, and I'm often reminded of Amy's birthday only after it's over. But decades of reminders in advance alert me to my mother's March 6 birthday—even now, several years after she's passed away. Our daughter Susan's St. Patrick's Day birthday poses no problem. However, my grandmother's birthday is a puzzler. Grandma Eddy, "Dolly," insisted that her birthday would be celebrated twice. She claimed not to remember whether it was March 13 or March 31, so she put a hold on both.

As for me, I was told that I was born just minutes before the Ides of March. I'm not sure what significance my parents placed on the Ides of March, but somehow they conveyed the impression that I was fortunate to have just squeezed in on March 14. In any case, by the time my birthday arrives, the weather in Michigan usually has thrown out a golf teaser or two. I used to fall for them and get out my golf clubs, only to see a few more weeks of cold, if not snowy, days. Now I don't fall for such tricks until mid-April.

One fine mid-April day in the year 2000 I decided to stop by Milham Park Golf Course, just to take a few swipes at the driving range. This year, for the first time in memory, I would start out the right way—practice before playing. I had only 45 minutes to hit, not enough time for a full round anyway. But, as I drove through the parking lot toward the driving range, I glanced at the first tee. It was beautiful and lonely. Soon I found myself striding toward that first tee, bag on my shoulder. Forty-five minutes was enough time for three holes, I said to myself, and golf is for playing, not practicing.

By the time I reached the tee, so had three others. We decided to head out together. A great way to start the golf season in the New Millenium, I thought. In fact, my first swing should be my first drive—no need for even a warm-up swing. Crack!! Not bad for a 59-year old, I thought, watching my drive soar down the right side of the fairway. Confident that the stiffness of my aging frame would ease off a bit after a 500-yard walk to the first green, I was already looking forward to my second drive.

The drive on the second hole was even better, 250 yards right down the middle. Then one of my playing partners, all of fifteen years old, rolled his drive just past mine. As we walked down the fairway, the young man commented, "Gee, that was pretty good. It looks like you haven't lost any distance in your swing yet."

Simply nodding my head and pulling my cap a little lower to conceal more of my gray hair, I vowed to myself to swing even harder on the next tee. Fading at fifty-nine? No way!

I had a belated thought the next day. Why hadn't I thought to say, "Listen kid, when I was your age, I was hitting them 300 yards. Look at your puny little drive, 251 yards with one of those high-techy monster drivers. You should have tried hitting with real woods like we did—not those fancy ones with gigantic metal heads. What an oxymoron, a metal 'wood'!"

Of course, since I was now using one of those high-techy monster drivers myself, exaggerating my past would have canceled his compliment, as did the fact that sometimes I actually did hit it 250 yards with my old persimmon woods. So, perhaps there was a little wisdom in my silent nod.

Golf Begins at Sixty?

It's a very pleasant mid-April evening, my car is cruising in the direction of Milham Park, and the sun won't set for an hour. I've been sixty for a month, and I haven't swung a golf club since last fall. The tenth tee is wide open. I decide that my first swing in this new decade will be the real thing—no practice swings. Boom! Right down the middle.

Thus began my first round of golf as a 60-year old. My second shot fell a few yards short of the green's tenth hole at Milham Park. I pitched onto the green and sank my putt for a birdie. Accustomed to starting off new seasons with bogies or worse, starting off with a birdie was a first for me.

A drive and an 8-iron put me 15 feet from the hole on the eleventh. Although playing alone, I broke into a grin. What if I started out with birdies on the first two holes? My putt rolled slowly toward the cup, lipped 180 degrees around the edge and stayed there. Easy par, nearly another birdie. I started joking with myself that maybe real golf begins at sixty.

My second shot on the twelfth ended up three feet from the pin. I sank the putt for another birdie. This is getting ridiculous, I thought—but fun.

I just missed a 20-foot birdie putt on the thirteenth, a short par 3. Two under par after four holes! This was beginning to get serious, and I could feel myself tightening up a bit. I topped my drive on the fourteenth, ending up only 75 yards off the tee. "At last," I thought, "I can still mess up." But I quickly returned to unreality by hitting a strong 3-wood and a good pitch, leaving me six feet from the hole. Unfortunately, I missed the putt, ending up with my first bogie of the evening. Still, I had recovered well from my terrible drive.

So, here I was on the fifteenth tee, 1 under par, a 60-year old very possibly playing his best nine holes ever, on his first round of the year! Then I realized it was nearly dark and that there was no way that I'd be able to finish the nine. What a turn of events.

I hit my drive down the left side, landing behind a tree. I clipped the tree on my second shot, leaving me a 9-iron from the green. I pulled my third shot into a sand trap. Faced with the prospect of a double bogie, I picked up my ball and walked back to the parking lot in the dark. A hole best left unfinished—and no doubt the same can be said for my round.

Slicing and Dicing

What a summer! A transcontinental flight to Vienna, a scenic trainride to Graz for a conference on philosophy for children, a delightful stop in Salzburg (featured by a dinner in Mozartplatzen, where I learned that Los Angeles had just suffered two earthquakes), an overnight run on the Orient Express (the train that's "always on time") to Paris, a wild taxi ride through Paris, necessitated by the Express' late arrival—only to arrive three minutes late for the train to Nantes.

The University of Nantes hosted the 1992 meeting of the Hume Society. A highlight was a visit to La Fleche, former residence of two great philosophers, the seventeenth-century rationalist Rene Descartes and the eighteenth-century empiricist David Hume.

Rescued from his hyperbolic doubts by the assurance that he had to exist in order to think, dream, hallucinate, or even doubt, Descartes attempted to follow his "light of reason" all the way from his celebrated, "*cogito ergo sum* (I think, therefore, I am"), to God and back to the general reliability of our senses.

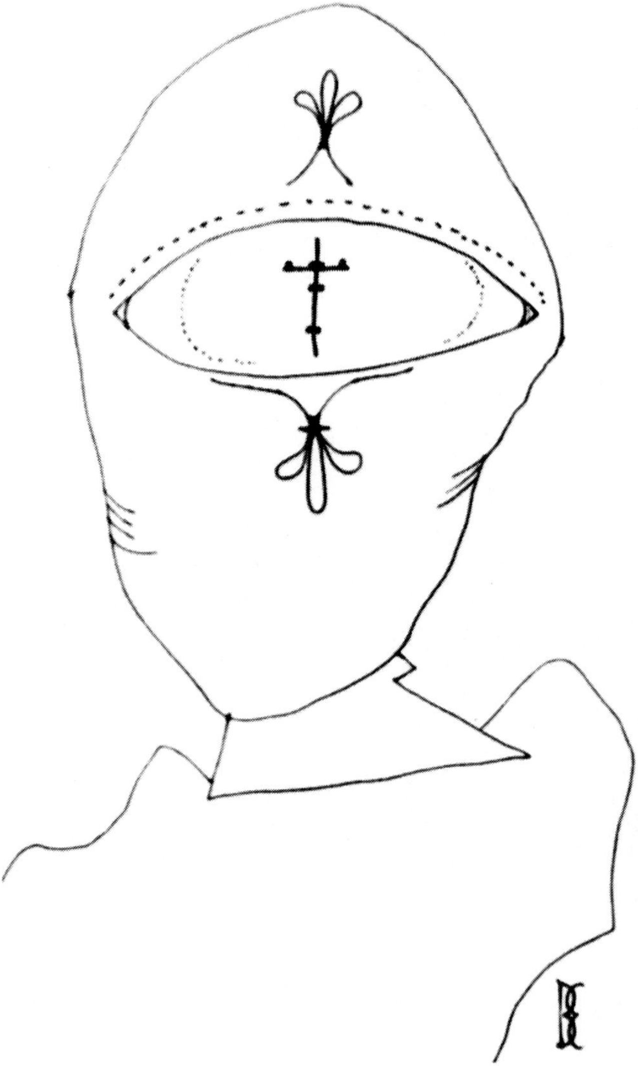

The Doctor

Hume wrote his reknowned Treatise on Human Nature in La Fleche, concluding that when he reflected on this self (Descartes' "I"), he ended in incoherence. At best, this self we experience is a bundle of momentary, separable perceptions—linked by causal relations of which we can have little understanding. Could the idea of the self's "continued existence through time" be a mere fiction of the imagination? ("Whose imagination?" the ghost of Descartes might ask.)

Heavy thoughts and heavy stomachs. The conferees were beset by a variety of intestinal disorders. Among the earliest victims was my good friend Wade Robison, President of the Hume Society. Suffering from diarrhea and cramps, poor Wade spent much of his day in La Fleche crouching on curbsides.

My version came later, a series of abdominal aches the likes of which I had never experienced. First fearing a heart attack and wishing to die back in good old Paw Paw, Michigan, rather than in a foreign land, I soon realized I was breathing too well for it to be my heart. For the others, the scourge quickly came and left—out one end or the other. For me, it was all an inside job that dogged me all the way back to Paw Paw and chased me up into the Rocky Mountains. Gallstones.

The best my gallows humor could muster up under attack was, "I leave no stone unturned." But now, after two months of misery, it was all about to end. What might I think about when stretched out on a bed outside the operating room awaiting the removal of my gallbladder? Well, I might recall all the golf gibes I've heard the past few weeks.

"How are your golf stones, Mike?"

"Okay, Stone, hit the ball." Or I might dip into the past and try to think of more Golf Lessons. For example, there was the summer I caddied at the Bloomfield Hills Country Club.

How *did* I muster up enough nerve to tell Mrs. Glenn Miller that she'd never reach the green with a 5-iron? I suggested a 4-wood and held my breath as she plunked it in the center of the green, thus earning me the privilege of being her regular caddy for the summer. Why *didn't* I ever ask her if she was related to *the* Glenn Miller?

How did I keep from laughing aloud when former Secretary of Defense Charles Wilson took a ten-inch divot that flew several inches straight up, landing in place with the ball virtually unmoved?

Do you suppose that the young tough who wanted to meet me in the caddyshack really would have whipped out his knife and threatened to carve me into little pieces?

"How'd it go?" boomed a doctor. Suddenly jarred back into reality, I was reminded of my circumstance. Lying helplessly in the crowded, noisy corridor outside the operating room, I wondered when the inevitable event would begin.

"A whole lot of slicing and dicing!" was the resounding reply. Not what I wanted to hear. Have these doctors no concern for the about-the-to-be-maimed?

"Good-bye Golf Lessons," I thought, "what am I supposed to think about now?"

"What'd you shoot," asked the first doctor, "a 42?"

"Yeah, but I was all over the place, slicing into the rough, slashing my way out...." A smile formed on my lips as I reflected on the irony of coming upon yet another Golf Lesson, in the hospital of all places.

"What would I be thinking now," I wondered, "if had no acquaintance with golf? Slicing into the rough, tangled mess of my abdomen!? Slashing his way back out!!? Dicing up my innards!!!?"

Finally Dr. Robert H. Hume arrived to give me final reassurances. Apprised of the occasion of the onset of my misfortune, and impressed by my Hume Society tee-shirt, Dr. Hume announced to the anesthesiologist that he was a member of the Hume Society. This, he said, was his philosophical thought of the day. I quickly commented, "I think, therefore, I am."

Why had such a thought occurred to me at this particular moment? Could those silly cartoons be right after all—the ones depicting one character saying, "I think, therefore, I am," while the second character is shown vanishing into thin air as his thoughts evaporate? Could my fellow fourth graders have been right when, challenging my vivid description of buzzing, whirring copper coils, they insisted that I *couldn't* have experienced anything when etherized while my broken arm was under repair? More slowly and falteringly, I added, "I'm about to be put to sleep, but I'll still *be*..., I hope."

"Without a doubt," replied Dr. Hume.

Keeping Up With the Joneses

"Don't worry, everything will be fine," said my good friend Jim Jaksa. "You'll probably even come up with a Golf Lesson from this—you seem to be able to get a Golf Lesson out of anything." This was on the eve of the removal of my gallbladder in 1992. Much to my surprise, I did come up with a Golf Lesson, "Slicing and Dicing."

Ten years later I had occasion to put Jim's remark to the test again. This time it was the surgical removal of a malignant "freckle" from my face. Bandage removed, I peered into the mirror to inspect my stitches. As if designed for a philosopher, they formed the shape of a question mark! But what is the question? How about, "What sort of hat should I now wear on the golf course?"

Sensibly enough, I decided to seek the advice of Dr. Karobin, the dermatologist who sculpted the question mark on my cheek. My first thought was that something like Greg Norman's full-brimmed cowboy hat would offer better protection than the standard front-brimmed types. "Good idea," commented Dr.

Karobin, "but I think you should go for an Indiana Jones hat."

What a terrific idea. Dr. Indiana Jones, hatless professor of archeology, donning his fedora to take on danger, intrigue, and the forces of evil. Dr. Michael Pritchard, hatless professor of philosophy, donning his fedora to take on tree-lined fairways, monstrous traps, and the seductive power of ponds. So, I bought my Indiana Jones fedora, vowing to break it in at the first sign of spring.

Meanwhile I decided to add more protection from the sun, a beard. "It gives you a professorial look," commented my colleagues. Hmmm—and what do you suppose I looked like during the first 35 years of my career as a beardless philosophy professor? "It looks distinguished," they added, carefully avoiding saying that it made *me* look distinguished.

"You look like someone famous, but I can't think of who it is," puzzled Cheryl McKinley, graduate assistant for the ethics center I direct.

"A famous philosopher?" I queried.

"Sean Connery!" she exclaimed. "That's who it is, Sean Connery." Sean Connery, Secret Agent 007? James Bond? Wow! No, Sean Connery, the bearded father of Indiana Jones in *Indiana Jones and the Temple of Doom*.

This was the second time someone compared me with Sean Connery. "How would you like your hair cut?" asked the hair stylist.

"With that growing bald spot on top, it doesn't much matter," I said. To which she replied, "I'll make you look like Sean Connery."

Okay, the aging Sean Connery it is. So what about the Joneses—Indy and his dad? To learn more about them, I had to rent the video. I knew that Harrison Ford's Indy is an Archeology professor. What about his dad? Well, he's a professor, too, with a doctorate in Medieval Literature. Still, maybe Sean Connery can play Harrison Ford's dad, but I can't. Harrison Ford and I are about the same age. Besides, I'm about to don Harrison Ford's fedora, not Sean Connery's scruffy little no-brimmer.

Furthermore, before he dropped out, Harrison Ford was a Philosophy major at Ripon College, where he was taught by my good friend Spud Hannaford, so I have more in common with Indy Jones than his dad.

But wait a minute. Why does Indy always get irritated when daddy calls him "Junior"? Does Junior mean that there are two Indy Jones? I'm a cross between Senior and Junior? Senior dons a beard, but no fedora. Junior dons a fedora, but no beard. I don both. The hat's a good fit and I like the beard, but will I be able to fill the shoes of either? More importantly, can either Indy break 80? And will fedora and beard help or hinder?

Whoops, Indy's daddy in William McKay's *Young Indiana Jones and the Circle of Death* is Dr. Henry Jones,. This would make him Henry, Sr., not Indy, Sr., and Indy must be Henry, Jr. Too bad.

But wait another minute. My grandfather, L.H. Eddy, was Lawrence Henry Eddy. So there are three Henrys here. Would all three call it, "cow-pasture pool"?

Mulligan Mike

It is nearly spring, and I've just turned sixty-two. It's too cold for golf, but not for softball—at least not for a softball batting cage, complete with a machine lobbing pitches my way. A nice warm-up for golf and softball, I think. Thirty minutes is enough. I feel pain between my shoulder blades, then in my shoulders. I've overdone it.

My evening is filled with recurrent episodes of pain and I wonder if I should call our doctor. I don't. The next day is pain-free. So is the next. However, on the third day the pain returns, again episodic, though less intense. The pattern repeats itself for the next several days. Finally I ask my doctor about what might be going on. "Could it be my heart?" I ask. He says he doubts that it is, but he'd be willing to see me the next day.

Dr. Shay checked my medical records, checked my vital signs, and administered an EKG. Still doubting that it was my heart, he nevertheless pointed out that at my age I'm in a higher risk group, and my

EKG showed a slight aberration. Would I like to take a stress test? Sure, why not.

Friday morning I took my stress test. Friday afternoon I was told that I flunked the test. Friday evening two of the main arteries to my heart were catheterized, "ballooned," and stented. Monday the same was done to the third. There had been significant blockage in all three.

As I waited for my Friday night entertainment, I reminded myself of Jim Jaksa's comment that I could probably find a Golf Lesson in almost anything. Where, I asked myself, was the Golf Lesson here? No answer. "Be patient," I admonished myself. "Let it come." I waited. Saturday and Sunday were filled with men's and women's basketball games on TV, but no Golf Lesson surfaced. Monday's procedure and another day in the hospital still left me without a Golf Lesson. Informed that all had gone well and that, by the way, I had not suffered a heart attack, I was sent home.

Could Jim have overestimated my imaginative abilities? Several days later I received a get-well card from my brother, Peter. The card was produced by the American Heart Association, and on the back it stated that, because of generous contributions and dedicated research, wonderful strides were being made in treating those with heart problems. Inside, Peter wished me well and added, "What a great Mulligan!"

Golf Lesson!

The Ghost of the "Goathills"

"You should do something you've never done before, something unique and out of the ordinary," suggested Cheryl McKinley, graduate assistant for the Ethics Center I directed. She knew that things had not been easy for me the past several months—a malignant "freckle" had been removed from my cheek, my wife Millie's memory problems had grown worse, and most recently I had three arteries to my heart catheterized and "stented." Clearly I needed some sort of change of pace.

Well, how about those 30-minute walks the heart rehab center folks were recommending? Without golf clubs? That would be unique, at least for me. As I set out on my first such walk, I thought some more about Cheryl's suggestion. She probably wouldn't think that a 30-minute walk quite did it. What else could I do?

Here I was, just walking around the campus where I had been teaching for 35 years. I noted how much had changed during that time—new buildings, sculpture works, flowers, and parking lots. I found myself standing on the edge of a large parking lot on the west edge of the campus. Somewhere in this parking lot was where we lived in the late 1960s. Gone were the homes that once dotted Steers Street. In fact, Steers Street itself was gone.

Our home was one of several owned and rented out by the university. It was just a stone's throw from the recently constructed Rood Hall where I taught all my classes. This is where we lived when our daughter, Susan, was born. It is where our son Scott, not yet four, taught himself how to ride a two-wheeler. He spent a full day getting on the bike, falling off, getting back on—until finally he could ride it in a circle. If Robert Gordon didn't need training wheels, neither did he. The fact that Robert Gordon was a year older and had a much newer bike didn't matter.

In mid-1970 we were told that we would have to move. The university needed to clear out its houses and put in a parking lot. We were told that we could buy the house at an excellent price if we had someplace to which we could move it. We had money for neither the house nor a place to put it. "How soon do we need to move?" I asked.

"As soon as you can," was the reply. "We need the parking lot by fall."

By fall the house was gone. In its place was a large hole where our basement had been. The hole remained there for at least another year. Finally it was filled to make room for a dirt parking lot. Several years later the area was finally paved, leaving no evidence of previous occupants.

Exactly where was our home, our yard, the big tree in the front yard, the passage through the back yard to Rood Hall? I couldn't be sure. I wanted to walk through our yard. So I began walking back and forth through the entire parking lot, making sure that, wherever it had been, surely I would have traversed some part of our yard.

As I continued my walk, I called Cheryl on my cell phone, described what I had done, and asked her if this qualified as something unique and out of the ordinary. She agreed that it did. Then I added something else.

I knew what had happened to our house. It was moved to Eleventh Street, between Parkview and Stadium, just a few miles away. For years it served as someone else's home. However, a few years ago it took on a new role—it had become headquarters for the Southwestern Michigan Alzheimer's Association, just about the time Millie began having serious problems with her memory. Recently we paid a visit to the Association, but in its newer location. Our old dwelling is on the market again.

I continued my walk. Suddenly I was standing before another parking lot. This one covered over what used to be a par 3 hole on the old "Goathills" golf course, all of which had been replaced by the university's West Campus. In fact, the Department of

Philosophy moved into a building just across the street from the last vestiges of that par 3 hole, shortly after we arrived in Kalamazoo. Traces of where the green had been were still visible then, and several of us practiced hitting short irons from the far end to that imagined green. But soon this area, too, paved the way to the future.

So, I had taken a 30-minute walk without golf clubs. But all along I had been wandering around the ghost of the "Goathills".

Pine Cones

Only once during our courtship years was I able to persuade Millie to join me on the golf course. Albeit reluctantly, she even took a swing with my 6-iron. "Nice hit!" I exclaimed as she made solid contact with the ball. "If you work at it, you could be pretty good at this game."

"That hurt my hands," she replied, politely handing my club back to me and firmly refusing to swing one ever again. In the more than 40 ensuing years she tolerated my fascination with the game, while effortlessly declining my occasional invitation to at least join me for a stroll around the links.

However, in the summer of 2002 Millie's resistance melted. It could be that her recent struggles with memory loss left her with no recollection of her previous indifference. In any case, as I eased the car off Lovers Lane into the entrance to the Milham Park golf course, she offered no protest. I quietly drove us toward the driving range. In the cool of early evening she commented on the beauty of the lush, green fairways. She laughed at the flocks of geese boldly walking onto the driving range, uncertain whether they were defiant or merely indifferent. She pointed to the low flying airplanes about to land at the nearby airport, warning, "Be careful, you might hit one of those planes with a golf ball."

"They're not anywhere near that close," I'd reply, flattered that she might even jokingly think that my drives could travel thousands of yards. And then there were the pine cones.

As I struck ball after ball, Millie gathered pine cones. Afterward, loading my clubs into the trunk, I commented on how I hit my irons or woods. Millie commented on the interesting features of the pine cones she placed beside my clubs. With pine cones as a lure, I was confident I could persuade her to pay a return visit to the driving range.

However, I've never been fond of going to driving ranges, especially when a real golf course is in full view. How, I wondered, could I ever persuade her to accompany me around the golf course? Even nine holes would be a long walk for her, and I always strongly preferred walking to riding in a golf cart, even when those I was playing with were riding. Millie might be willing to walk a hole or two, but that would be it. Her hip would begin to bother her, just as it does when taking long walks on the beach in the uneven sand.

Finally, it hit me. Some golfers can't walk the distance, but rather than give up the game, they ride.

Faced with such a choice, what would I do? Would I ride or quit the game? I'd ride, of course, but wasn't that my situation now?

Leaving Millie alone in order to go to work was one thing, but to do so to play golf for a couple of hours was quite another. She needed my company, and she depended on me to help her find enjoyable things to do. She thoroughly enjoyed long rides in the countryside. How about some rides in a golf cart?

To my delight, Millie said yes. Nine holes at a time was just right. Some real golf for me, a nice ride in a beautiful setting for Millie. She commented on birds, flowers, cloud formations, and even saw the humor in shots bouncing off trees or splashing into ponds. Whenever she'd see me on the edge of losing my temper, she'd laugh, remind me that it's just a game and tell me I shouldn't take things so seriously. And then there were the pine cones.

The holes with pine trees were her favorites. By the end of the summer, splendid collections of pine cones were displayed throughout our home. Why this fascination with pine cones?

One of my former students, Nick Sousanis, suggested a mathematical connection. Pine cones, like pineapples, many flowers and many, many other natural phenomena illustrate the Fibonacci Spiral. The Fibonacci Spiral can be constructed from a complicated set of connected squares, the sides of which are, proportionately, the successive numbers of a Fibonacci series. Quarter circles are then drawn in each square, beginning with the smallest, and connected at the corners between squares of consecutive Fibonacci numbers! The resulting spiral can easily be seen in beautiful conch shells.

Ah, you ask, what is a Fibonacci series of numbers? The series begins 1, 1, 2, 3, 5, 8, 13..., and each number is the sum of the two preceding ones. A famous mathematical problem illustrates this series: How many pairs of rabbits will there be a year from now under the following conditions? Two rabbits, one male and one female, are born on the first day of the year. It takes a rabbit one month to reach sexual maturity; and the gestation period of a rabbit is one month. After reaching sexual maturity, female rabbits give birth every month to exactly one male and one female rabbit. No rabbits die within this year.

Even though she aced all her math courses and she was a librarian, I doubt that Millie has ever given any thought to Fibonaccian math. Leonardo Da Vinci did, however. He was as fascinated with math and science as he was with art. In fact, he thought his Vitruvian Man was perfectly proportioned, based on his understanding of the Fibonacci series as represented in the Golden Ratio. Of course, Millie must have learned something about Da Vinci in her Humanities 101 at Alma College, and she's undoubtedly seen pictures of his Vitruvian Man. But I doubt that she connected this with the math that so fascinated Da Vinci.

So, Millie's attraction to pine cones must have another source. It could be simply their natural beauty— for they are beautiful—one needn't be a math genius to appreciate this. However, there is another possibility, one that I cannot confirm but enjoy contemplating.

A quarter century ago I went on an early spring golfing escapade with my brother and several of his buddies. We spent several days on Jekyll Island along the southern coast of Georgia. While trying to avoid alligators in the rough, I couldn't help but notice the largest, most gorgeous pine cones I'd ever seen. I thought Millie might enjoy them, too. So, I filled the pockets of my golf bag with pine cones and presented them to her on my return.

I know Millie enjoyed those stunning pine cones. Aside from that, I think she was pleased that, even when waging battle on the golf course with my brother and his friends, I was thinking of her. Could this have had something to do with her willingness to accompany me to the golf course 25 years later? Another kind of Golden Ratio?

Play It As It Lies

In the course of our phone conversation, my brother Peter asked, "How's Millie doing?"

I replied that there were no dramatic changes to report. She was simply continuing her struggles with memory loss and confusion. We just have to make the best of whatever's there for us, I said.

"Yes, you have to play it as it lies," offered Peter. Realizing he was quoting Bobby Jones, the greatest amateur golfer of all time, he added, "There's another golf lesson."

"Right," I agreed, "I guess it is." But just *what* is the golf lesson here?

Bobby Jones was talking about the integrity of the game of golf. Allegedly, he lost a tournament because he inadvertently moved his ball in the rough. Although he was the only witness, he didn't hesitate reporting that the ball moved and taking a two-stroke penalty. Cheating was not something he could tolerate.

"You have to play it as it lies," no matter how it gets there, where it ends up, or whatever the cost.

Of course, not all golfers display such integrity. One can cheat one's way around the golf course—improving one's ball in the rough (or fairway), not counting all one's shots, giving oneself four-foot putts, and so on.

However, Bobby Jones is remembered for more than his golfing integrity. His health took a cruel turn. He suffered from syringomyelia, a degenerative disease of the spinal cord. Still, he was, as golfing great Sam Snead described him, "a model of strength, fortitude and dignity." Although unsure that it is a true story, Snead recounts an incident in Bobby Jones's later years. An old friend visiting Jones was so upset by his condition that he began to cry. Jones responded, "Now, now. We won't have that. We are supposed to play our ball as we find it."*

* Sam Snead, "Play It as It Lies," in Jack Canfield, Mark Victor Hanse, Jeff Aubery, and Mark & Chrissy Donnelly, eds., *Chicken Soup for the Golfer's Soul.* Deerfield Beach, FL: Health Communications, Inc., 1999; 162.

Keep Walking

A few days after our mother passed away, my brother Peter and I found ourselves puzzling over one of her drawings, a peculiar little piece she'd hung in her sun-room. We examined the outline of a rather grotesque looking cat.

Its huge head stares out with green, penetrating eyes. It possesses a lean, powerful nose and a grin-and-bear-it smile wider than its face. A few strands of hair stream from its back. Tattooed on its side is a painter's pallet and a flower. In place of back paws is a large black, high-heeled shoe. Above the cat's head is the caption, "Keep walking."

"What's this all about?" we asked. It could have been her Picasso, we mused. Most likely, she was making a statement about her feet. As her family and friends knew, Elly's feet had bothered her a great deal in recent years. At first it was only a seasonal affliction. Eventually she soaked her feet in water several times a day to find relief, and she went shoeless as much as possible.

Eurythmalogia was the Mayo Clinic's diagnosis, she told us, "Hot burning feet—throbbing, itching, swollen, beet red," is how she described it. Not life-threatening, but no known cure; this was something she simply had to live with. She resolved to grin-and-bear-it, and to *keep walking*.

No doubt Elly's cat is taking a stand against eurythmalogia. However, its unyielding eyes suggest much more to me. They prompt a set of recollections.

I am nine years old, positioned in center field, waiting for the opposing softball *team* to take its turn at bat. As usual, we are behind ten or so to nothing. Suddenly my eight teammates stalk off the field shouting, "We quit! We quit!" A real-life Charlie

Brown, I refuse to leave the field. Running through my head is one of my mother's first lessons, "The world can't *stand* a quitter."

I am fifteen years old. I get no joy from running cross country, but I'm doing it to get in shape for basketball. Much as I dislike running a race, what I dislike even more is the thought that I might not finish. So I pace myself, dropping to the back of the pack—but still running. Near the end, gasping for breath with side aching, I'm ready to stop. But Elly's admonition rings in my head, "The world can't *stand* a quitter." The end in sight, I pick up my pace and sprint to the finish line.

I am still fifteen years old, sitting on the end of the bench, my high school basketball team trailing by 20 points or so. Only two minutes are left, and maybe I'll get my chance to play. Elly is there to the end. She's upset—not because we are hopelessly behind, not because I'm still on the bench, but because people are leaving and the game isn't over. The players haven't quit; neither should the fans. To this day I find it nearly impossible to leave an athletic event early, no matter how settled the outcome.

I picture my mother's long, looping golf swing. "Sweep the club like a broom," she says. Klump, klump, klump—one bad shot after another. Why not quit? Never.

"The world can't *stand* a quitter. Besides, there's always the next shot, and it might be great. That's what brings you back." In any case, she says, the bad shots aren't her fault—it is, as she puts it, her plagued (pronounced, "play-ged") driver, 3-wood, 5-iron, 9-iron, or putter.

Golf reminds me of the Myth of Sisyphus. Sisyphus is doomed for eternity to roll a rock to the top of a hill, only to have it roll back down again, roll it back up.... Doomed for eternity to hit a little white ball—again and again and again—to no avail. But if only Sisyphus took time to look at that hill a little more closely, he would notice fine differences. Each roll of the rock is slightly different than the others. A twist or turn here or there might result in a record low number of complete revolutions of the rock to get to the top of the hill. And there are the surroundings—blue skies, grey skies, wind, rain, sleet, snow, flowers, bushes, trees, sand traps.... Anyway, you have to *keep walking* —if you don't, you'll miss all the high points. Besides, the world can't *stand* a quitter.

ACKNOWLEDGEMENTS

I would like to thank my uncle, Bret Eddy (1913–2000), for the illustrations in this book. Although he worked as an accountant for more than 40 years for General Electric in Detroit, his first love was art. More than 70 of his paintings hung in GE offices while he worked there. Many of his paintings were also exhibited in a variety of galleries, including some in New York City and the Detroit Art Institute.

However, as a young man he had thoughts of becoming a cartoonist. He drew cartoons for his fellow GE employees, on the occasion of birthdays, retirements, and other celebrations. He also filled more than 100 stenopads with humorous drawings. These passed into my care, and I have selected a few for inclusion in this book. Although he certainly did not have my *Golf Lessons* in mind when he drew them, I'd like to think that he would find their placement among my stories appropriate.

I am indebted to my mother, Elenore Parshall, for the illustration on the back cover. Sister of Bret Eddy, for years she admired his art work, as we all did.

At age seventy she decided to become an artist herself. Her painting "Keep Walking" was, I am sure, a personal statement about coping with some of her physical discomforts late in life. But her many other works of art amply testify to the joy she took in life, whatever obstacles it might present.

I thank Diane Worden and Holley Lantz for their expert editing and graphics assistance.

Finally, I thank Rich Baldwin for his friendship, and his support and encouragement in helping me share these stories with others.

To order more copies of *Golf Lessons: Links to Life,* by Michael S. Pritchard

Discounts: Available for multiple orders and to retailers. For rates, contact Buttonwood Press at RLBald@aol.com or phone (517) 339-9871.

Fax orders: (517) 339-5908

Mail to: Buttonwood Press
P.O. Box 716
Haslett, MI 48840

Each softcover copy is $19.95 $ ___________

Shipping and Handling:
Book rate is $3.00 for first book
and $1.00 for each additional book. $ ___________

Tax: Add 6% sales tax for Michigan
residents (for one book, $1.20). $ ___________

Total: For one book, this is $24.15 $ ___________

Please make check payable to: Buttonwood Press

PLEASE PRINT

Name: ______________________________

Address: ______________________________

City: ______________________________

State: ______________ Zip: __________

For additional information and other available titles, visit the website of Buttonwood Press at www.buttonwoodpress.com

Thank you!